BECOMING SONS OF GOD

BECOMING
SONS OF GOD
Learning the Art of
Living Life to the Fullest

ROBERT STONE

DESTINY REFORMATION MINISTRIES
TULSA, OKLAHOMA

Becoming Sons of God
First Edition, 2010 by Destiny Reformation Ministries

Unless otherwise noted,
all Scripture quotations are from

THE KING JAMES VERSION

Scripture taken from
THE NEW KING JAMES VERSION
© 1979, 1980, 1982
Thomas Nelson, Inc. Publishers.

Scripture taken from THE MESSAGE,
Copyright © 1993, 1994, 1996, 2000,
2001, 2002. Used by permission of
NavPress Publishing Group

Scripture quotation taken from the
HOLY BIBLE NEW INTERNATIONAL VERSION
Copyright © 1973, 1978, 1984,
by International Bible Society.

Scripture taken from THE AMPLIFIED® BIBLE
Copyright © 1954, 1958, 1962, 1965, 1987 by
The Lockman Foundation. Used by permission.
(www.Lockman.org)

ISBN # 1453774688 — EAN-13 # 9781453774687

Published in the
United States of America by
Destiny Reformation Ministries
PO Box 330118
Tulsa, OK 74133

Printed in the
United States of America by
Create Space
A division of amazon.com

OTHER BOOKS BY ROBERT STONE

Ordering Your Steps
Gifts From the Ascended Christ
The Principle of Twelve; The Pattern of God
Finding Financial Freedom
Pursuing Perfection

I continue to be so grateful to the Holy Spirit for His
continuing revelation of the Kingdom of Heaven
and the Abundant Life to be found and lived.

The Lord is establishing truth in a new and dynamic way.
I am amazed at the process and purpose to which the sons
of His Majesty have been called and chosen.

I dedicate this book to my wonderful children;
Talitha, the one most like me.
Tanyka, the merry traveler who goes with me.
Tyler, who will go beyond where others have never gone before.
And...
The spiritual sons given to my life by our
Gracious Heavenly Father

Contents

FORWARD

Throughout my lifetime and ministry I have seldom heard anyone even mention, let alone write or teach on the supernatural principle of scriptural sonship. Because of this God's people, for the most part, have missed out on the essence of what sonship was meant to be: *the art of becoming*. Under the Holy Spirit's direction I want to share that it is only through the advent of biblical sonship that anyone will find the catalyst for manifesting the tremendous promise given to Abraham in Genesis 12:2-3.

"I will make you into a great nation and I will bless you; I will make your name great, and you will be (become) a blessing. I will bless those who bless you, and whoever curses you I will curse; and all peoples on earth will be (become) blessed through you."

Without hesitation I can say the biblical principle called *"sonship"*, is the foundation for our becoming and will empower anyone to live life to the fullest.

I can promise that by following the principles of this book incredible blessing will begin flowing to and through your life. There will be a powerful impartation of faith and confidence. This impartation will enable you to envision the very picture of your future that God has placed within you. Then as the sonship principle takes root, the Holy Spirit will inform, instruct and impart God's glory into your life. You are about to become something more, something special, and something extraordinary.

This book is not a just a sonship book, but through it you are about to become the best son you can possibly be. This is not a business book, but as you begin to grow and mature, your business will increase and expand beyond your current imagination.

Beginning with the first page your inner self will sense yourself...becoming. Following after the process set forth on these pages will cause you to experience life as never before. This becoming follows a unique pattern. There will be the "enduring" phase, followed by the "embracing" segment and then concluded by the "enjoyment" period. Each one will move you toward the story God wrote about you from before your birth. (Psalm 139) Supernatural revelation and motivation will take you from wherever you are to where you have always wanted to be.

I can promise you that the journey before you will exceed your wildest expectations and give you the strength to reach your fullest potential. Your life is about to take on new purpose and accomplishment. This is your time. Line by line and precept by precept a life of happiness and fulfillment begins today! You are about to *"become a wonderful son in whom God is well pleased!"*

INTRODUCTION

In my book *The Principle of Twelve, the Pattern of God* I wrote much about the Lord Jesus Christ being the *Pattern Son.* He is the Only Begotten of the Father, full of grace and truth. For anyone serious about becoming all they can possibly be, the Lord Jesus Christ is *The Pattern* for their thoughts, attitudes, actions and habits. In fact it was when the early church followed this pattern that the world came upon the idea of calling believers "Christians" which meant to be *"like Christ."* Yet, as we enter the second decade of the twenty-first century there is a tremendously ever growing spread of beliefs of what it means to *be Christian.*

As never before, people from every continent are growing more independent in their perception of spiritual ideas and concepts. This independency has greatly influenced most modern believers, pastors and churches. The majority of younger people have now independently chosen certain pieces of scripture, and interpreted them through not only certain held traditions flowing out of a previous move of God's Spirit but out of new age concepts like those of Maxwell Maltz or L. Ron Hubbard. The resulting interpretations are a mixture of combining scriptures, traditions, ideas, and new age concepts. This has created a new "picture" of who Jesus Christ is. This new picture and pattern has then influenced almost every believer's view on what it means to be a Christian (like Christ).

Modern theology has made Jesus Christ more guru than God. This picture of *The Christ* has caused some believers to focus on Jesus the miracle working purveyor of good news while others now see Him as an advocate of "going green." Still others center their attention on His theological teachings and if they were correctly or incorrectly interpreted by the early church fathers in the light of modern philosophy. Some only call Him Savior while others speak of Him as Healer of sickness and Deliverer from bondage. Others proclaim emphatically Him as the Baptizer in the Holy Spirit. Almost all hail Him to be their "soon coming King."

The majority of these spiritual pictures have their basis in past awakenings, revivals or spiritual outpourings. The greatest theological differences between believers coincide with certain theological and philosophical revelations given to men the likes of Martin Luther, John Calvin, John Wesley, Charles Finney, William Seymour, Billy Graham and Kenneth Hagin.

Over the last five hundred years these revelations have created distinct schisms within the body of Christ. From these revelations, men have desperately worked to categorically define their particular theology. Emphatically, churches and believers currently characterize themselves as Universal, Unitarian, Traditional, Reformed, Evangelical, Fundamentalist, Holiness, Pentecostal, or Charismatic. (Of course this is not close to an exhaustive list.)

One aspect I have found disturbing is the fact that almost all Christians have pushed the idea of the Kingdom of heaven off into a far distant future. This has been caused by most Christians aligning themselves directly or indirectly with basically one of two different theological views of the Scriptures. These differing and quite opposite views are known as *Covenant Theology and Dispensationalism.*

The standard description of Covenant Theology views the history of God's dealings with mankind in all of history, from Creation to Fall to Redemption to Consummation, under the framework of three overarching theological covenants—the covenants of redemption, of works and of grace.

Covenant Theology is not merely treated as a point of doctrine, but it is viewed as the structure by which the biblical text organizes itself.

As a framework for biblical interpretation, Covenant Theology stands in contrast to the other main theology of the day, dispensationalism. The differences between the two are founded on distinct differences in regard to the relationship between the Old Covenant with the nation of Israel and the New Covenant in Christ's blood. Regarding the theological status of modern day Israel, Covenant Theology is often referred to as "super sessionism," or "replacement theology." This is due to the perception that the theology teaches that God has abandoned the promises He made to the Jews and has replaced the Jews with Christians as his chosen people in the earth. Almost all Covenant theologians deny that God has abandoned his promises to Israel, but see the fulfill-ment of the promises to Israel in the person and the work of the Messiah, Jesus Christ and His Church.

Dispensationalism, on the other hand, is a theological view of history and biblical interpretation that became popular during the 1800's and early 1900s and is held today by most conservative Protes-tants. It supplies an interpretive grid for understanding the flow of the Bible as a whole, and is frequently contrasted with its opposing view of Covenant Theology. The fundamental difference is the relationship of God with the nation of Israel on one hand and the Christian church on the other.

Dispensationalism divides the ages and the way God chooses to work with mankind within those ages. These divisions have laid a foundation for cessation theology. Simply put, dispensationalism says that there are certain offices like the apostle and prophet are no longer needed in the body of Christ and have passed away. Also, there are certain gifts and manifestations, like speaking in tongues which God used in the first century, but have ceased due to the interpretation of Paul's words to the Corinthians; "These will cease, when that which is perfect has come." (1 Corinthians 13:10)

Dispensationalism is a form of premillennialism. Premillennialism sees the past, present, and future as a number of successive administra-tions, or "dispensations" (Ephesians 3:2 KJV), each of which emphasizes aspects of the covenants between God and various peoples at various times. Consequently, it places a heavy emphasis on how God deals with certain people at certain times in certain ways. It also has a strong emphasis on prophecy and eschatology, known as the study of "end times."

Both of these theological views, the revelations given to past people of God and the interpretations of those revelations have created divi-sions that seem to be similar to the divisions found in Paul's first letter to the Corinthians where he wrote;

> *My brothers, some from Chloe's household have informed me that there are quarrels among you. What I mean is this: One of you says, "I follow Paul"; another, "I follow Apollos"; another, "I follow Cephas"; still another, "I follow Christ." Is Christ divided? Was Paul crucified for you? Were you baptized into the name of Paul?*
> (1 Corinthians 1:11-13)

Thankfully, over the past two decades I have seen something very small and wonderfully unique emerging. Yet, like the spiritual reforma-tions of the past, its development has been labeled as "not from God, off track, and at times heretical." Some have called it, *The Theology of the Kingdom* (also called Kingdom Now by its aggressive antagonists) and have tried to make it into no more than a revival of *The Latter Rain Movement of the 1950's*. It also has in some ways been connected to C. Peter Wagner's understanding termed, *The New Apostolic Reformation*. *The New Apostolic Reformation* has been viewed as a short lived movement in Protestant Christianity (1990's) that grew out of the Pentecostal and Charismatic movements. Believers in the *Latter Rain and the New Apostolic Reformation* have generally asserted that God is currently restoring the lost offices of church governance, namely the offices of the Prophet and the Apostle. Also, by restoring these offices, God is building a spiritual kingdom in the lives of His people which is being ruled by the present and living King, the Lord Jesus Christ.

Great attack has been leveled at those like Wagner and others. I have seen one major problem has been the lack of character and integrity among the sons of these movements. Another problem has sadly been that many pastors suddenly became "prophets" when "prophets" became a fashionable term in the 1990's. Then, many of these "prophets" became "apostles" when it seemed as though the prophets would have to submit to the apostles that were showing up. Others began teaching about "spiritual fathers" only to twist a scriptural truth into a way to make more money or manipulate those they were leading. A following for many of these people has developed because of so many dear folks are so hungry for God and that they are willing to do just about anything.

The truth about the Kingdom of God teaching (just like Evangelical Fundamentalists and Pentecostals believe) is that the Church is the true body of saved believers. Most teachers of the Kingdom (like Myles Munroe) generally hold to the Pentecostal belief that believers who are "baptized in the Holy Spirit" are enabled to "speak with new tongues." (Acts 2:1-4; Mark 16) *The Theology of the Kingdom* also maintains the need for the restoration of all Church offices (Ephesians 4:11-16) and the need for the scriptural character manifested in the lives of church sons. These sons, who are seen as ordained by God, are given power and authority by God to lead by serving, as described in the biblical letter of the apostle Paul to the Ephesians. As such, this theology believes in the 5-fold offices of the Church; of which the Prophet and Apostle has been absent from the Church for the last 2000 years, and are now being restored.

Sadly, the lack of character in many sons (concerning money, systematic theology and manipulative leadership) has left what I believe began as a true move of God in shambles. The worldwide recession has put an end to the prosperity that was promised. Sadly, there are now millions of people who can only see the bad and have chosen to "go back".

The Holy Spirit has convinced me that I was to begin teaching and writing about the true *Theology of the Kingdom*. I believe God is still seeking to see spiritual reformation within the church on a global scale beginning first with the local church which is then to be networked to other likeminded churches. Adherents to this theology should begin seeking to relate to one another as one body and focus on being completely submitted to Jesus Christ, who they see as the head of the Church. The Holy Spirit is calling believers and churches to develop at their core a heart focused on taking the gospel of the Kingdom to the nations of the earth. (Matthew 4:23; 24:14)

In this book I intend to show you from the scripture that the ministry of the Church should not be concerned with membership numbers but rather with a process referred to as *the formation of Christ within its members.* (Galatians 4:19) Included in this theology is a strategic commitment to New Testament/Apostolic Church government. Like Paul's vision for the church, congregations should consist of dedicated believers; who all function and carry weight in the church; working together toward the commission and vision of the Kingdom of God.

The sons of God in these churches must believe in exhibiting the characteristics of *"servant sonship."* They should lead by example, never asking others to do what they don't do or have not done themselves. The focus of such sons should be to take care of people, teach them, train them, equip them, challenge them, prepare them and send them out to do the work of the ministry. I believe that with the development of the five-fold ministry gifts in this type of church mentality, God will be able to prepare His people spiritually, mentally and physically so that they might go into all the world and "make disciples of all nations." (Matthew 28:19)

This "making of disciples" is philosophically connected to the reception of the Spirit of adoption in Romans 8:15-23. And this philosophy is directly connected to the pattern Jesus used in the development of His disciples as seen in the gospels. This process is best illustrated in "The Sermon on the Mount." During His short homily Jesus told His young listeners:

"Be perfect, therefore, as your heavenly Father is perfect."
(Matthew 5:48)

In New Testament Greek the word "*perfect*" is usually illustrated in the word *teleios*. This Greek verb primarily means, "To having reached the end," "term," "limit," and therefore it is generally translated as being, "complete," "full," and "perfect."

The adjective, *telaios*, is used in scripture to describe heirs being of age, people who are seen by others as mature. It also is used to portray full grown trees or something in good working order or condition. When applied to the believer the word refers to one who is spiritually mature, complete and well rounded in both character and behavior. Examples are,

> *Jesus answered, "If you want to be perfect, go, sell your possessions and give to the poor, and you will have treasure in heaven. Then come, follow me."* (Matthew 19:21) NIV

> *Let us therefore, as many as be perfect, be thus minded: and if in anything ye be otherwise minded, God shall reveal even this unto you.* (Philippians 3:15) KJV

Teleios is translated "mature" in the New International Version of Ephesians 4:11-13

> *"It was he who gave some to be apostles, some to be prophets, some to be evangelists, and some to be pastors and teachers, to prepare God's people for works of service, so that the body of Christ may be built up until we all reach unity in the faith and in the knowledge of the Son of God and become mature, attaining to the whole measure of the fullness of Christ".*

I understand that all the previous and current revivals, reformations and revelations given to God's people have been and continue to be for the purpose of our *becoming the sons* (John 1:14) and the *perfecting of the saints* (Ephesians 4:12 KJV).

In the current move of the Holy Spirit there is great temptation by the movements of the past to pigeon-hole the new reformation theologically. To do so will again mean rejection by the majority of the body of Christ. God's current move should be seen as a new empowering by the Holy Spirit for the Church to reach it's fullest of potential. God has not changed His mind. He is the same; yesterday, today and forever. He desires that every human become all they can be. Such "becoming" can only be realized in no other name, but the Name of Jesus. (Acts 4:12)

Looking back, Methodists have been known because of their "method." Baptists rightly have the reputation for "baptizing." Pentecostals have traditionally been tagged as "those people who speak in tongues." In the early years of these movements there was much emphasis on people becoming what God wanted them to become. But none of these previous moves of God, at least over the last several years, has produced a way of thinking where God's people are focused on "becoming." (1 John 3:2)

Our God's glorious presence and power can best be experienced in our *becoming the sons of God*. This *becoming* is what this book is about. It is the will of God for each and every life. *I pray you begin becoming today!*

CHAPTER ONE

Preparation

Inquisitive. Irritated. Inspired. These are a few of the responses the Baptist elicited. Throughout Jerusalem and Judea the buzz was all about him. There hadn't been this much excitement in the City of God since King David brought the Ark of the Covenant into Zion a millennium before. Like David's emotional outburst that day, the Baptist's preaching was part political rally, part street carnival, and part old time tent revival.

There was much more to the Baptist than what first appeared. Without references, recommendations or resume he had stepped forward like the prophet Elijah from obscurity into the public eye. His method was simple. His voice pierced heart and soul. He was a man sent from God. Heaven's newest ambassador, exploding with tremendous passion, preached much more than the normal modern sermon. His clothes, his voice, his urgency screamed that John the Baptist carried a divine prophetic mandate. He saw himself in tune with a preceding prophet who had declared his prophetic word hundreds of years before.

I am a voice of one calling: "In the desert **prepare** *the way for the LORD; (Or A voice of one calling in the desert:* "**Prepare** *the way for the LORD) make straight in the wilderness a highway for our God. Every valley shall be raised up, every mountain and hill made low; the rough ground shall become level, the rugged places a plain. And the glory of the LORD will be revealed, and all mankind together will see it.* (Isaiah 40:3-5)

The Baptist's prophetic words thundered across the philosophical and theological landscape. His preaching seemed more political than theological, even revolutionary. When asked if he was the promised

Messiah, John's voice rose to a fevered pitch. His dark eyes flashed with excitement. He was only a voice, nothing more, nothing less. Yet his voice was for one thing: *to prepare the way for our becoming.*

John the Baptist ministered in the genre of the prophets of old who had gone before him. He was a spokesman, a voice crying in the wilderness, speaking into the desert of religiosity, expressing God's heart to the place of prophetic desolation. The prophet's viewpoint was that spiritual decay was leading God's chosen people into an unholy abyss. He was convinced that God had sent him as like a medieval crier to declare the soon appearance of the King of Glory.

In preparation for the Messiah's promised appearance John preached a unique message of repentance that confused the politicians and infuriated the religious sons. John's message of change was not about making converts to a certain philosophy within the bounds of Judaism. Nor was his prophetic ministry about gathering a group of blinded and fanatic followers to himself. The Baptist wasn't seeking alliance with the factions dividing the Sanhedrin. In fact, when he saw many of the Pharisees and Sadducees coming to where he was baptizing, his voice thundered with incredible authority:

"You brood of vipers! Who warned you to flee from the coming wrath? Produce fruit in keeping with repentance." (Matthew 3:7)

In the midst of his preaching, baptizing and disciple making John the Baptist focused his message on one thing...*becoming.* His intensity focused on The Word *becoming* flesh as the Son of Man, but also on men *becoming* sons of God.

His concentration was quite different than others of his day. He saw monumental change coming in the realm of the Spirit. This change would flow out of the door called the incarnation. As God's seer, the Baptist saw the Word *becoming* flesh as the catalyst that would result in the fulfillment of the original plan and purpose of God.

God's begotten Son would be *becoming* the Savior of the world. The result would be people who would be begotten of God and therefore becoming the children, the offspring, the family, the sons of God. The four hundred year old spiritual vacuum was about to be filled. The Baptist understood that a radical change was about to take place not seen on the earth for a thousand years.

The prophets who preceded him declared themselves and all of the Lord's people to be nothing more than the servants of the Lord (Psalm 90:13). But the Baptist's preaching involved a new ideal. Rather than people being servants, God's people would *become* His sons. Starting with spiritual rebirth, they would be transformed from the inside out. Such transformation would result from a change in the way one thought (repentance), followed by the supernatural impartation of God Himself into the heart and mind (regeneration) which would result in their *becoming* the sons of God.

Why shouldn't he believe this? His birth had been nothing less than a miracle. The angel of the Lord had appeared to his elderly father and promised a son, a special son. The angel said this unique son should have a new name, John. The name John is based in the Hebrew word, *channah*, which when translated means "grace." John was sent from God to begin the glorious message of the grace of God to all men.

John also came in the spirit and power of the great prophet, Elijah. He was the one to fulfill Malachi's prophecy of turning the hearts of the fathers to the children and the hearts of the children to the fathers. Zachariah's son became the forerunner of the promised Messiah of mankind. He would precede the Rock, the Shelter, the Strong Tower, Isaiah's prophesied Emmanuel.

Led by the Spirit of the Lord God, John had begun his public ministry. No doubt, that even before he began preaching his message of repentance John wondered about many things. He wondered about his call. He wondered about the future. He wondered about the Roman occupation. Who was the Messiah? Would the Messiah overthrow the Romans and set up His own government? How was he was supposed to re-present Him?

His preaching was outside the accepted norm of the local synagogue elders not to mention the religious crowd from Jerusalem. First, his clothes were made of camel's hair, and he wore a leather belt around his waist. Included in his diet were locusts and wild honey. John's spiritual perception was sharp. His faith was extreme. His passion unbridled. He seemed to be on the fringe of what was and wasn't religiously acceptable.

Preaching the need for supernatural change, John's message rang clear, *"Repent (change your thinking), for the kingdom of heaven is here."* People from everywhere went out to see him. They came from Jerusalem, Judea and the whole region surrounding the Jordan River Valley. In response to John's powerful prophetic message they confessed their sins and were baptized by him in the Jordan River.

Given the nickname "the Baptist", he immersed each of his converts in the Jordan waters as an initial sign of their *"becoming"*. John saw baptism as a prophetic picture. Those who believed his message and were baptized were leaving their past through a kind of spiritual death and were being raised to a newness of life. Each then was taught to see themselves as choosing to *become* something and someone different and better than their past. They consecrated themselves waiting for the appearance of the coming Lord from glory.

This was and is the first step toward supernatural reformation. The Baptist's disciples took the first baby steps to overthrowing the so called "servant" mindset that had and has infiltrated the understanding of God's people. From the beginning God had wanted sons not servants. He longed for a family, not religion. Religion was man's way of trying to reach God which made trying to be a servant of God seemed philosophically logical. The word that came to John caused him to see things differently. Like Elijah he saw things in great upheaval in the Spirit.

He saw that the heart of man had become dark and decadent. God had revealed to him the power that is experienced when people choose the light. God's powerful prophet knew that he was not the light; but that he came only as a witness to the light. Speaking of time and space from the viewpoint of eternity, John declared that the one that would come after him had already surpassed him because that One (the Messiah) had existed before him.

John's ministry was as reforming as the revelation written by Moses hundreds of years before. The revelatory words are in the first lines of the Torah. *"The earth was (became) without form...And God said, Let there be (become) light."* In a spectacular vision Moses saw God's power in His re-creation of the heavens and the earth. That which had de-formed over millions of years was re-formed by the spoken word.

This vision came months after Moses had experienced the supernatural power of God at the burning bush. There on the backside of the wilderness, his shepherd's staff "became" a serpent. Then when he followed Jehovah's instructions, the serpent "became" a staff. The Lord proved His power to Moses when his hand "became" leprous and then "became" well again. All of this had taken place as a demonstration to define the Name of the Lord; I AM or I WILL BE WHAT I WILL BE. Apparently, God wanted Moses to know that He possessed the power to cause things like the bush, the staff, his hand and even his very life to "become."

Returning to the creation vision, Moses saw that with each spoken word, the creation "became." When writing about it Moses used the Hebrew verb *hayah*. (Genesis 1:2). *Hayah* means "to come about, occur, take place, arise, appear, *to come into being or become*".

First, Moses saw light *be-coming* out of the darkness. With each spoken word from the voice of God everything made *became* from something else. The sun, the moon and the stars materialized from the firmament. The mineral, vegetable and animal kingdom started *be-*

coming one proceeding from the previous. Moses stood on the revelatory bridge spanning time and eternity and watched as God finished His glorious reformation of the earth. When all seemed finished, Adam was formed from the dust of the earth and God breathed into him and Adam *became* earth's first living soul. (Genesis 2:7)

The Baptist was like Moses in another way. He was God's first prophet in over four hundred years. Like the deliverance of Israel from Egypt, John could sense that the coming of the Messiah would open a new chapter in the species of humankind.

The curtain hiding the mystery of the ages was about to be torn asunder. Something absolutely glorious and unbelievable was about to be revealed. He didn't fully understand that within his own family a virgin had conceived and had given birth to a son. The son wasn't just any son. The son was God's Only Begotten Son. Unbeknown to John, the Son of God had been hidden among his own relatives. Just as Psalm 68:6 says, *"God had set the solitary one in his family."* God's Son had been concealed in the obscurity of a tiny Galilean village not far from where John's ministry was reaching its zenith.

Years passed. These years were but a moment compared to the millenniums God had been working to put the plan of redemption in order. God and His Son had long waited for this appointed time. The Word, The Logos, The Eternal Essence of God Almighty had become flesh and was about to step out of the shadows onto earth's grandest stage. As morning became afternoon God's Son, the Alpha and Omega, Beginning and the End kissed his mother Mary goodbye and strode confidently toward the Jordan. The Son was none other than John's first cousin, Jesus of Nazareth.

The creator had *become* the creation. The Word had *become* flesh.

And the reason? Initially, so that the whole creation could be set free. The curse of sin would be broken. Mankind would be redeemed from the presence, power and penalty of sin. That which had been lost would be recovered. (Luke 19:10) The Kingdom of God would be established on the earth. The Son of God would open the doorway between time and eternity so that every man, woman, boy and girl could by faith be given the power to *become* the sons of God. These sons would be re-born and re-generated. They would be born from above and then begotten by the Father Himself. These sons would be infused with supernatural DNA and be given the right, the authority, the opportunity and the power to *"become the sons of God."*

It is time for this mystery, this hidden wisdom to become known again. (1 Corinthians 2:7) God desires that all humanity would come to repentance. (2 Peter 3:9)

From the moment of our conception, before the moment any of us takes our first breath, there is a voice divinely instilled within all of us. This voice is the person God created us to be. This voice is crying to *become*. It is the desire of every heart to become more today than yesterday. When we learn to crawl, we want to walk. When we walk, we want to run. After learning to run, we want to jump. As children we want to become teenagers and as teenagers we want to become adults.

This *"becoming"* fills our thoughts and imaginations from the moment we take our first steps. From their teen years many seek to "find themselves" through nature, philosophy, religion and education. Others exhaust themselves physically, financially and emotionally seeking to find the path, the way or the track through life that would cause the "becoming" part of their heart to be filled. That emptiness can only be described as the hope that someday, somehow and in some way they will…*become*.

The voice within us is like The Baptist's voice. It is the voice preparing us for the arrival of the King of Glory.

This is the generation of them that seek him that seek thy face, O Jacob. Selah. Lift up your heads, O ye gates; and be ye lift up, ye everlasting doors; and the King of glory shall come in. Who is this King of glory? The LORD strong and mighty, the LORD mighty in battle. Lift up your heads, O ye gates; even lift them up, ye everlasting doors; and the King of glory shall come in. Who is this King of glory? The LORD of hosts, he is the King of glory. Selah. (Psalm 24:6-10)

Yet, there seems to be almost no prophetic voices declaring it is our time to *"become."*

The Baptist knew. He knew that the will of God for this blue planet was to become a tribute to God's majesty, power and glory. He also knew that God's Son, the Lamb, and Eternal Lord would become flesh so that we who are born flesh and blood could become more than teachers, firemen, doctors, or housewives. John knew that through the power of the Spirit of Jehovah all of us could become the sons of God.

Such a transformation can and will only be found as we follow the example of two of John the Baptist's disciples (Andrew and John). They were given an invitation to follow the King of Glory. They were given opportunity to the process of becoming followers first, then disciples, later apostles, but most importantly, sons of God.

*The following day, John was again standing with two of his disciples. As Jesus walked by, John looked at him and then declared, "Look! There is the Lamb of God!" Then John's two disciples turned and followed Jesus. Jesus looked around and saw them following. "What do you want?" he asked them. They replied, "Rabbi", "where are you staying?" "**Be-coming and you will see,**" he said.* (John 1:35-39)

CHAPTER TWO

The Word Became Flesh

"And the Word, entering a new mode of existence, became flesh, and lived in a tent [His physical body] among us"
John 1:14 Wuest Translation.

Zebedee's youngest son and the Baptist's closest disciple stood in awe as his mentor's cousin came off the bank of the river and into the water. The water splashed and the sand swirled up from the river bottom. Jesus of Nazareth moved confidently through the water toward them. It was as though time stood still. The Baptist seemed moved beyond anything his young disciple had ever seen. The Baptist trembled. He cleared his throat in preparation of the word that started coming up from his belly.

John the Baptist realized that the prophecies spoken by Isaiah and Jeremiah were literally moving toward them in the flesh. His own prophetic statements from the day before were still ringing in his own ears. He couldn't believe the words were about to come to pass so soon and right before his very eyes. Unbelievably the Messiah, the Savior of the world, stopped just a few feet away. The Baptist didn't know what to do at first. Should he bow his knee? Declare God's praise? Introduce his disciples? Give thanks? Should he speak or be silent?

"John, I need you to baptize me." Jesus began. A somewhat awkward response tumbled off the Baptist's lips. "Not me. Are you kidding? I didn't realize that YOU were the Messiah. I am not worthy to untie your sandal. Anyway, why does the King of Glory need to be baptized?" (Matthew 3:14)

"Order must be accomplished," Jesus replied. Nervously the son of Zebedee (John the disciple) and the other disciple, named Andrew, waited in awe realizing The Messiah, The Christ, The Lord stood within arm's reach. The water felt different. The clouds above stood still. They were focused on what was happening below. The birds, the wind, the sky, in fact all of creation seemed to be quietly standing at attention. This was the moment they had been waiting for...for a long, long time. This was the moment that The Son of God would open the door for the manifestation of the sons of God.

Since Adam's fall all of God's creation had longed to return to its original condition and purpose. Because of the first Adam's rebellion the creation had deformed and over time been devoured and in many ways destroyed. Earthquakes, hurricanes, drought, pestilence, and flood had brought much agony to the lives of the earth's inhabitants. Yet as Jesus of Nazareth turned so the Baptist could immerse Him...the creation seemed to be holding its breath. The planet itself remembered that, from a previous moment of time, God had spoken.

"I have placed a curse on the ground. All your life you will struggle to scratch a living from it. It will grow thorns and thistles for you, though you will eat of its grains. All your life you will sweat to produce food, until your dying day. Then you will return to the ground from which you came. For you were made from dust, and to the dust you will return." (Genesis 3:17-19)

But God had spoken through another prophet. Isaiah had given the planet hope.

"For, behold, I create new heavens and a new earth: and the former shall not be remembered, nor come into mind."
(Isaiah 65:17)

In that prophetic moment the Creator's words were supernaturally imprinted, imparted and imposed upon the planet's chaos. The planet remembered how that in the Genesis account, suddenly and then slowly the planet...*became*. Yes, nature remembered that the *"becoming"* that turned chaos into order was short lived. From a perfect garden the first man refused the responsibility of establishing God's Kingdom on the earth and along with his wife, committed treason. This act of immorality resulted in all of the creation having to painfully suffer through the curse that came with mankind's fall from innocence. The creation had groaned continually as it waited for the manifestation of the sons of God. (Romans 8:19)

Now the creation had reason to hope again. The All Powerful King of Glory, The Creator of all things created, The Word who was with God and was God from before the beginning began, *had become...flesh*. Some thirty years earlier during the Feast of Tabernacles angels had brought the good news of the Christ child being born in the tiny town of Bethlehem. Simple farm animals watched as Mary gave birth and then placed the child in a manger. Shepherds who were keeping watch over their flocks by night joined the celebration because of angelic visitation. They hurried to stand at the feeding trough where the baby Jesus slept.

That Word in the flesh now stood in the same river where time had stood still hundreds of years before. Following Joshua's orders the priests had stepped into the Jordan and the water had rolled back all the way to the small city of Adam. The wet sand beneath His feet was the same sand that watched as Elijah and Elisha walked across on dry ground. This river, the Jordan, was where Naaman's leprosy had been wondrously cleansed away.

The Messiah's voice flowed articulately and with authority. He again told the Baptist to baptize Him.

The Lord God Jehovah, the Timeless One, Wonderful, Counselor, Mighty God, Everlasting Father, Heaven's Glorious Lord, and Eternity's God Almighty submitted to scriptural order for the purpose of setting the Pattern for the millions of sons to come. He, The Christ, who was legally the son of Joseph of Nazareth, had to "die" to His legal position and then "be born" into His rightful place as the Son of God.

The Baptist placed his rugged hands on the head of Jesus and gently put Him beneath the waters. For a few seconds Jesus knelt beneath the top of the water. At that moment in time the Eternal One *became begotten*. He then came up and out of the waters praying. A glorious thing happened. (Luke 3:21-22) As Jesus prayed, the heavens were opened, and the Holy Spirit descended in a bodily shape (like a dove) upon him, clothing Him with heaven's mantle, and a voice came from heaven, which said, "*Thou art my beloved Son in Thee I am well pleased*". (Matthew 3:17KJV)

Have you never wondered why the voice spoke directly to Him, informing Him of His Sonship? Didn't He know who He was? Of course He did. Hadn't He told His mother eighteen years earlier that He needed to be about His Father's business? But then, why was He informed of His Father's thoughts?

Nothing happened by accident in the life of Jesus. Every detail was ordained before the foundation of the world. This was a momentous day in His life, and great things were happening in that day both in heaven and in earth. Some have taught that the Father was simply bringing forth a milestone in the earthly ministry of Jesus the Prophet. Theologians have questioned if the Father's words were for the benefit of those who were standing nearby or perhaps they were for our benefit.

From scripture the Father spoke because it was the completion of His Son's adoption. In Hebrew thought a male child was circumcised on the eighth day. This made the son heir to the covenant of Abraham. (Galatians 4) When a Hebrew son was twelve he went through a ceremony where he was "apprenticed" to the business that belonged to the father. (Luke 2:49) This apprenticeship initialized the son's adoption. Eighteen years later, the Israelite son was then given the keys (Matthew 16:19) of his father's business thus making the adoption and inheritance complete.

But it was more than that. As a chasm stood open in the sky above them, the voice of the Father who had spoken over the Son identified Him as "my beloved Son." The Baptist heard the glorious voice, and at the same moment, saw what appeared to be a dove. He saw the dove "clothe" the Son. This was similar to Elijah casting his mantle on his spiritual son, Elisha. It was a momentous occasion for the Baptist, his disciples John and Andrew, as well as the Son of God, let alone the whole world.

The words the Father spoke that day are similar to the prophetic declaration of Psalm 2:7;

> *"I will proclaim the decree of the LORD: He said to me, 'You are my Son; today I have become your Father.'"*

And akin to the voice at the transfiguration;

> *"A voice from the cloud said, 'This is my Son, whom I love; with him I am well pleased. Listen to him!'"* (Matthew 17:5)

Years later the writer of Hebrews used these words to show that Jesus Christ was the expressed image of God;

> *"So Christ also did not take upon himself the glory of becoming a high priest. But God said to him, 'You are my Son; today I have become your Father.'"* (Hebrews 5:5)

I want you to imagine the baptism of our Lord with me. Jesus came up out of the water, dripping wet, the river water ran down His face mingling with the hot tears flowing from His eyes. Jesus turned toward the bank. The prayer began under the water continued. Heaven's Eternal Word was praying as none who stood on the river bank had ever heard. His prayer was different than the prayer of Moses (Numbers 11:2), Elijah (1 Kings 18:36), and Hezekiah (Isaiah 37:16). He didn't pray as a priest, a prophet or a king. Jesus prayed as The Son of The Eternal Father. He prayed as The Prophet, The Priest and The King all at the same time.

At that moment, the whole world began experiencing both God and man in a new mode of existence. Where in times past faith was toward God, now the sons of God would have opportunity to live by the faith of

God. (Galatians 2:20) Where in times past the High Priest would enter the Holy of Holies "for" them, now this new High Priest would enter the Holiest Place "as" them. What Glory Divine! What Majesty on High!

The Father was pleased. The Word *became* flesh. The Word wrapped in real humanity *became* The Son. All of this so we could *become the sons of God!*

What a story to tell to the nations! I love to tell this story! The story of Jesus and His love!

The Son of God had spent His first years as a child in Egypt before moving with His earthly parents to the tiny Galilean village of Nazareth. For thirty years He had quietly lived outside life's spotlight. He had been faithfully establishing righteous customs and habits in His own life. He now would be the example for others to follow.

For years Jesus had been growing, physically and mentally waiting for this day of His adoption, or "His Father's placing Him as a full grown mature Son." Galatians, chapter 4, tells how that the heir, (though he is Lord of all) still has to be treated as a servant while he is a child, living in his immaturity. So it was that Jesus, in fulfilling the pattern for His Body, had to go through the same process. And it was in reality, not a hypocritical sham or token event. This all actually took place, and were very real events in the life of our Lord all for the purpose of our *becoming!*

Jesus, the firstborn of His Father, had been tenderly cared for and watched over - not only by His Father, but by all the angels as well. The angels knew that Jesus of Nazareth would inherit all of His Father's possessions and become the Master of all. But, in the care of an earthly mother and adoptive father, a discipline was involved. The child was not given all of his Father's authority, nor was He allowed to have His own way or choose his own course.

He learned to do as He was told, to be obedient even to those of less stature than He was to become. As Clarke's Commentary says concerning Galatians 4:1; "Though he be appointed by his father's will, heir of all his possessions, yet till he arrive at the legal age he is master of nothing and does not differ from one of the common domestics."

Jesus had submitted to Joseph, his adoptive father, whom God had set over Him. He had been quietly working and preparing to enter into and establish The Father's business. Now the time had come for Him to be revealed as the Pattern Son. From this moment on He would heal the sick, raise the dead and set the captive free. He would now take the first of His steps toward accomplishing the complete will of The Father.

"In the beginning was the Word, and the Word was with God, and the Word was God. He was with God in the beginning. The

Word became flesh and made his dwelling among us. We have seen his glory, the glory of the One and Only, who came from the Father, full of grace and truth." (John 1:1-2, 14)

There is no argument within these words to prove the existence of God any more than in the Genesis account. John's gospel simply states that the Word exists and is without any doubt He is the Creator of the universe. John reaffirms that the Word, as Creator, stepped out on nothing, made somewhere, hung it on nowhere, told it to stay there, and it stayed.

Using the Greek words *"logos eimi"*, John's gospel states the Word's continuous and timeless existence (the Word was). This existence is best related in the words spoken by the angel of the Lord from Moses' burning bush translated I AM or I WILL BE WHAT I WILL BE. This is quite different from the Greek words *"logos sarx egeneto"* (the Word became) used in verse 14 to describe the incarnation of the Son of God.

The term *Logos* is applied to Jesus Christ only in John 1:1,14; Revelation 19:13; and 1John 1:1. While existing eternally with God and as God, the Logos was and is in perfect relationship with God. This is a relationship of equality and intimacy, i.e., face to face with each other. John writes without reservation the pre-existent Eternal Logos *"became flesh"* (*sarx egeneto*). The Almighty One literally transformed Himself from *"being to becoming"* and from *"creator to creation"*. God Himself moved from eternity to time and from heaven to earth. He chose from being the Word to becoming the Only Begotten Son.

He who is...*has become. He became so we could become.*

John wants us to know that the power that creates and sustains life in the universe is the Logos. From the Logos "all things came into being." Creation is thus presented as a becoming (*ginomai*) in contrast with being (*eimi*). This *"becoming"* is a result of the Logos being the transitional agent in the work of creation. Like the author of Hebrews who names God's Son as the one *"through whom he made the ages,"* the Logos becoming flesh is John's explanation of the creation of the universe. He wants us to know that *"the all things were created in him"* (Christ) and *"all things stand created through him and unto him"*.

John does not here say that the Logos entered into a man or dwelt in a man or filled a man. The Word *became* Man. Trying to explain the exact significance of the Greek word *egeneto* in this sentence is beyond the powers of any language. The Logos simply *"became"* dwelling or pitching His tent among us. His earthy created tabernacle is the result revealing God's Shekinah glory here among us in the person of God's Only Begotten Son. John insists that in the human Jesus the created and the creation has the opportunity to behold the Shekinah glory of God who was and is the One who existed before with God.

John clearly wants us to experience and encounter the manifested glory of the Word in The Son, Jesus Christ. Because *The Being became* we who believe on Him are given the right and power to become what we were not before. In the full spiritual sense, we who believe have been given the power to *"be-come"* a new mode of existence. This new mode of existence is called a "son of God."

"Those who are led by the Spirit of God are sons of God. For you did not receive a spirit that makes you a slave again to fear, but you received the Spirit of sonship or adoption. And by him we cry, 'Abba, Father.'" (Romans 8:14-15)

In eternity past the Logos was not seen as or understood to be, The Son. But Isaiah prophesied concerning the incarnation, *"a child (the creation) is born, a son (the creator) is given."* (Isaiah 9:6) The Son was given from human pre-existence. The pre-existent Word was only Spirit until He became the Son of Man living in and as flesh.

We have the opportunity to *"become the sons of God"* because His *"becoming"* opened the door. The Word (without any limitation) became (in a body with limitations) so we who by sin were born with extensive limitations are given the right and power to become God's sons living without any limitation.

"...because as he is, so are we..." (1 John 4:17)

"Jesus beheld them, and said unto them, With men this is impossible; but with God all things are possible." (Matthew 19:26)

"If you can believe, all things are possible to him that believes." (Mark 9:23)

Because of the incarnation we are able to *BECOME* a new existence. As sons of God, Christ makes His appearance first to us, and then in us and finally through us. This is what the Kingdom of God is about. By faith we enter into a state of being not known to us before. This faith establishes a foundation for a new existence.

"Therefore if any man be in Christ, he is a new creature: old things are passed away; behold, all things are BECOME new." (2 Corinthians 5:17)

The Lord Jesus Christ as the *First fruits* establishes the pattern of life for us to become,

"But now is Christ risen from the dead, and BECOME the firstfruits of them that slept." (1 Corinthians 15:20)

"Yet to all who received him, to those who believed in his name, he gave the right to BECOME children of God" (John 1:12)

CHAPTER THREE

Invited to Be-Coming

"Be coming," he replied, "and you will see."

The two disciples were amazed at the events that surrounded the baptism of Jesus of Nazareth. Still trying to grasp the enormity of the manifestation of God's glory they and their mentor, the Baptist, saw Jesus walking nearby the day after His baptism. The Baptist pointed toward Him and said, "Behold the Lamb of God." The Prophet then predicted and portrayed the Messiah as the Lamb of God who would take away the sin of the world. He also identified Jesus of Nazareth as the One who must increase as his ministry decreased. Andrew and John took him at his word and acted on it. They came running after Jesus and He turned hearing their hurried steps behind Him.

Jesus asked, "Is there a reason you are following me?" They responded by addressing Him as "Rabbi" or teacher and asked where Jesus was staying. Jesus answered with a polite invitation and a future promise. *Be coming and you will see.* This is the first part to the complete invitation given later to Nathanael in John 1:51,

> "I tell you (the Greek is plural) the truth, you shall see heaven open, and the angels of God ascending and descending on the Son of Man."

The invitation Jesus gave John and Andrew was one of *be-coming*. Becoming a son of God initiates the ability to see spiritually. Like the Greeks in John 12:21; in our becoming we should see Jesus.

Something great is happening. You have chosen to make it this far in this book. Evidently you are choosing to become. In the days and weeks ahead God will be drawing you to the place of laying down your life, i.e., the "old" nature. The Adamic nature must be put to death. This is something true for all those who are called into this High Calling and who choose to be conformed to His Image. The events at the Jordan River represent death and resurrection. Baptism is the antitype of Old Testament circumcision. In baptism there is a burial of all that remains of the old life. The flesh is cut off. Legally one dies to everything former. In the coming out of the water there is a resurrection into His divine life. It is a picture of being born again. The Word of God is clear. In our becoming we shall see Him. Each step forward illuminates our understanding.

We see this in Peter's explanation found in 1 Peter 3:18-22,

"The like figure (antitype) whereunto even baptism doth also now save us (not the putting away of the filth of the flesh, but the answer of a good conscience toward God), by the resurrection of Jesus Christ: Who is gone into heaven, and is on the right hand of God; angels and authorities and powers being made subject unto him."

Theologically speaking, our spirits were dead in trespasses and sins (Eph. 2:1) so when we come to the saving knowledge of Jesus Christ, believe with our heart and confess with our mouth, our spirit man is released from the prison of sin or brought from death unto life (resurrected), but it is our soul (mind, will and emotions) that is saved (present tense) and continues to be (being) saved (perfect present tense).

Baptism is the antitype. Each of us like Noah has been immersed in water until all that was is gone. Noah's salvation came by water as does ours. Jesus said,

"I tell you the truth, no one can enter the kingdom of God unless he is born of water and the Spirit." (John 3:5)

This is part of Peter's theology. In Acts 2:38, *Peter replied,*

"Repent and be baptized, every one of you, in the name of Jesus Christ for the forgiveness of your sins. And you will receive the gift of the Holy Spirit."

When we present ourselves as a living sacrifice, no longer being conformed to this world, but being transformed by the renewing of our mind, we then are able to see through the eye of faith. We see Jesus just as He is, in all of His splendor and glory. We also hear the Father's voice declaring our sonship and adoption. God our Father declares that we are His. We no longer belong to ourselves, but to Him. There can be no partial percentage for the be-coming. Jesus must *be-coming* Lord of your life.

At the Jordan Jesus laid down His earth life and put Himself completely into the hands of the Father. His will had become completely swallowed up in the will of His Father. He became a vehicle of expression for Father God. God may reveal His might and power in the hurricane or the lightning. He might express His creative ability in the great Milky Way. But only in Jesus, His Son, did The Father first truly reveal and express His own divine nature.

So the Son, as a human laid down His own rights, His own thoughts, His own will, and became a visible means of expressing that which was divine, that which was invisible. Now all of mankind can see what God is really like. Jesus is the One to truly represent Him, the One to express His love and compassion and wisdom and humility, as well as His authority and dominion in heaven and earth. God in Jesus has one like Himself, in His own Image, and He publicly declared Him as His Only Begotten Son.

The true nature of Jesus Christ must be manifested through us to a world full of unbelievers. To them He is invisible; they will not read the Bible to learn about Him. Their thoughts are continually on other things. But He seeks a Body, a Corporate Son, in which He can eternally express His own Nature. Like John and Andrew, those without Him are very close to His heart. He is wooing them, drawing them, bringing them to a place of laying down their own lives and partaking of His divine nature. For you see, His Body is His Corporate Body, it is made up of a multitude of called, chosen and faithful sons.

This is the essence of our beginning. This is the first steps to becoming. It is the choice to be made into His Image. Yes, it is sometimes a difficult road. For you cannot take our old life or self into a new mode of existence. We need Him to do it. The Father desires that like The Son we become a vehicle of expression for Him. We find this example in the church at Thessalonica.

*"And so you **became** a model to all the believers in Macedonia and Achaia."* (1 Thessalonians 1:7)

The life of the Thessalonians had changed dramatically. From the first visit of the Apostle Paul their life in Christ was not merely the formation of some religious habit. Life flowed from their constant communion with the Holy Spirit. The activities of eternal life were quickened and maintained by divine strength, and by keeping their eyes constantly fixed upon the object of faith, the Word who became flesh. Their becoming the Body of Christ was embraced, endured, and enjoyed.

At first, it was a time of discipline, child training, and learning. Through Paul's ministry the believers in this Macedonian city began by learning obedience to God's principles and humility. Later, Paul wrote to them to encourage them. *"For as you begin this journey of "becoming", you will need encouragement from the Lord, the scriptures and other believers."*

Let's look at the becoming that took place in the Thessalonians in line with what our Lord Jesus said in Matthew 13. When good seed is planted; there are different rates of productiveness. Some bring forth 100 fold, some 60 fold, and some 30 fold (Matthew 13:8, 23). The quality of the seed cannot be brought into question here for the seed is the Word of God. But the difference in the harvest has to do with what the good ground does with the seed. And all born again believers who choose to become sons of God produce His likeness in some form and dimension.

I want you to hear the invitation God is speaking to you. He desires your becoming a son of God and to come into the complete image of Jesus Christ (Romans 8:29, John 1:12). He longs to bear His likeness in the 100 fold realm. There is a call in your heart for you to be God's highest and best. Do not settle for less.

A true son of God will not be satisfied with less than God's best. The 30 fold speaks to us of those who choose to stay in spiritual infancy. Such folks remain in the elementary teachings of Hebrews 6:1-2. These people love the Lord, are going to heaven, with the life of Christ within them. But they never experience more.

The 60 fold is the double portion, the Spirit-filled life, walking in the supernatural of God, manifesting the fruit and gifts of the Spirit. It is the place of divine anointing. It is the church in the first chapters of the book of Acts. It is a glorious experience and a beautiful walk in God. But it is not the fullness. It is not the complete will of God.

The one hundred fold is the number that speaks of completeness. The fullness of Christ-likeness is found in this dimension. This is adoption. It is Christ being formed within. It is full sonship. It is simply becoming a complete image of the Lord Jesus Christ, in the full meaning of the term. God's remnant has never settled for less.

To the hundred fold son of God, just getting into heaven is not good enough. These committed sons are not excited by the prospects of a mansion just over in the glory land. There are many who like the sound of nice sounding songs, a white robe, a halo and a star in one's crown, but that is not what God has planned for you! Becoming is about pressing to come into the measure of the stature of the fullness of Christ. To *be filled with all the fullness of God* (Ephesians 3:19) must become your goal. I can promise you nothing else will satisfy your soul.

Abraham saw a City, whose builder and maker is God, and from that time on, nothing else mattered to him. He didn't waste time trying to build his own city. What he had seen was far beyond the efforts or dreams of men. So he waited for God to bring him to it. He counted himself a pilgrim and stranger on this present plane of life, because he was a citizen of a higher order. True sons of God are of like spirit. Those who embrace the *becoming principle* will not settle for what they possess now, though it seems safe and good, and presents no immediate dangers. They are willing to risk danger, trusting in Him, to whom they have committed all things, which they might gain all that He is and has for them.

I want you to be encouraged to move forward in your becoming a son of God. The word *encouragement* means to: inspire with hope, to support and to stimulate. Encouragement comes more readily to those who embrace excellence. Our God is an Excellent God. His Name, His Will and His Way are Excellent. Excellence is a picture of life in the hundred fold way of life.

"O LORD our Lord, how EXCELLENT is thy name in all the earth!" (Psalm 8:1)

"How EXCELLENT is thy loving kindness." (Psalm 36:7)

"Praise him for his mighty acts: praise him according to his EXCELLENT GREATNESS." (Psalm 150:2)

The Father desires that we like the Thessalonians become a model of excellence. A model is the picture of what inspires others to become. For if the model is not excellent, what will people be inspired to be. How does one inspire someone to become more than they are? By showing them that they are the model or example for others to follow and by telling them there is room for improvement. (1 Cor. 4:16)

Encouragement also means to support with an expectation of help. Paul told the Thessalonians;

"Wherefore when we could no longer forbear, we thought it good to be left at Athens alone; And sent Timothy, our brother, and minister of God, and our fellow laborer in the gospel of Christ, to establish you, and to comfort you concerning your faith." (1 Thessalonians 3:1-2)

He reminded them that they were not alone. Paul, Silas, Timothy and most of all, the Lord Jesus and the Holy Spirit were on their side, wanting to bring help in their time of need. Like a father he no doubt taught them that, *If God be for us, who can be against us?* (Romans 8:31) He also helped them to understand that *the weapons of our warfare are not carnal, but mighty through God* (2 Corinthians 10:4). He taught them to know that *our God is able to do exceeding abundantly above all that we ask or think, according to the power that is at work in us.* (Ephesians 3:20)

CHAPTER FOUR

Finding Your Be-coming Identity

"And lo a voice from heaven, saying, This is my beloved Son, in whom I am well pleased."

The first obstacle I see in the lives of those who hear the message of the Kingdom is dealing with their false identity. Sadly, most believers believe that they are inadequate and unprepared to become the person God has called them to be. Like the picture of Moses standing before the burning bush, many are afraid and are tempted to turn away from the plans God has for them. God told Moses and the Israelites that before they could come into their promised inheritance they needed to come out of their previous way of living and thinking.

Moses and most of Israel had developed a false identity. They saw themselves differently than Jehovah saw them. Sadly, having a false identity is a diabolical landmine that the enemy plants to *keep us from becoming* the person that God wants us to be.

What causes someone to be stuck even when they want more than anything else to become the person of their dreams? Many times it is a result of feeling inadequate. One of the primary reasons some people feel inadequate is because they grew up in an insecure environment. Their world seemed very unpredictable, and there was an uncertainty to life that prevented them from feeling safe. Their parents may have had problems such as alcoholism, drug use, or they may have left home or died when they were very young. These create an atmosphere of instability.

This is very different than how the Lord is. He is predictable, faithful, and unchanging. The Bible says,

"Jesus Christ is the same yesterday, today and forever." (Hebrews 13:8)

And that,

"God is not a man, that he should lie, nor a son of man, that he should change his mind. Does he speak and then not act? Does he promise and not fulfill?" (Numbers 23:19)

Also,

"Because of the LORD's great love we are not consumed, for his compassions never fail. They are new every morning; great is your faithfulness." (Lamentations 3:22-23)

It was feelings of being inadequate that caused the thinking that desperately needed changing in Moses and the Israelite nation. The children of Israel saw themselves lacking and unable to become the people God told them they could be. The descendents of Abraham, Isaac and Jacob could not see themselves as the sons of God who had the promise of becoming the conduit that God would use to bless all the peoples of the earth. Four hundred years of slavery had produced a slave mentality. They were consumed with a severe sense of lack in every area of their lives.

We can see this by looking at the story of Moses sending twelve spies into the Promised Land to see what was needful for Israel to possess the land. For several days they traversed the land seeing the goodness it possessed. Yet instead of focusing on the power God had shown in their deliverance from Egypt, the goodness of the land and the Word of the Lord they focused on who they weren't and could not do.

Numbers 13:27-29 tells us,

"They gave Moses this account: "We went into the land to which you sent us, and it does flow with milk and honey! Here is its fruit. But the people who live there are powerful, and the cities are fortified and very large. We even saw descendants of Anak there. The Amalekites live in the Negev; the Hittites, Jebusites and Amorites live in the hill country; and the Canaanites live near the sea and along the Jordan."

Instead of seeing the blessing, the majority of these men could only see the trouble. They couldn't see the opportunity, only the obstacles. Even at one point ten of their sons declared that they were nothing more than grasshoppers in the eyes of their enemies. (Numbers 13:33) Evidently, the sons of God were dealing with false identity.

The sons of God saw themselves as slaves. This slave mentality caused them to embrace doubt instead of faith and problems instead of possibilities. Generations followed in their steps. False identity also revealed itself in Samson, Gideon and the first king of the nation, Saul.

Centuries later the nation of Israel was still dealing with their identity as a nation and as individuals. The Lord spoke through His prophet Isaiah who declared the vision of who the people were and who they were to become;

> *"Fear not: for I am with thee: I will bring thy seed from the east, and gather thee from the west; I will say to the north, Give up; and to the south, Keep not back: bring my sons from far, and my daughters from the ends of the earth; Even every one that is called by my name: for I have created him for my glory, I have formed him; yea, I have made him."* (Isaiah 43:5-7)

False identity must be overcome if we are to become the sons God has planned for us to be. We are sons of God by the act of believing and receiving, (John 1:12) which results in our new birth. Believing on the Lord Jesus Christ and receiving eternal life is required to begin the process of becoming a son of God. We must first believe that Jesus is the Anointed One who has come from God.

The Greek phrase that speaks to our believing combines both the present and perfect tense:

> *"Whoever IS BELIEVING that Jesus is the Anointed One, has been born of God."* (1 John 3:5)

Another example is when Jesus said in John 8:31,

> *"If ye CONTINUE in my word, then are ye my disciples indeed."*

Some people think all that is required in becoming a son of God is a moment of faith. But true sons have faith from the point of salvation onward. Sons of God will manifest that they have been first born and then begotten of God by continuing to believe in God's Eternal, Only Begotten Son, the Lord Jesus Christ.

First John 5:1 states that a person who is born of God believes that Jesus is the Christ. He must believe that Jesus the man is God incarnate--the Messiah, King, Savior, Redeemer, and the center and focus of revelation.

First John 5:4 further defines the concept of faith:

> *"Whatever is born of God overcometh the world; and this is the victory that overcometh the world, even our faith."*

"Believe" and "faith" are two English words for the same Greek word in two different tenses. (pistas, and pisteuo)

The initial ingredient in the becoming life of the son of God is his faith. Our victory is based on the reality that Jesus Christ is who He claimed to be and who we become through our continuous faith in Him.

In the New Testament the Apostle Peter wrote concerning the identity of God's people;

> *"But ye are a chosen generation, a royal priesthood, an holy nation, a peculiar people; that ye should show forth the praises of him who hath called you out of darkness into his marvelous light: Which in time past were not a people, but are now the people of God."* (1 Peter 2:9-10)

The Lord desires for His sons to realize that their lives are not based upon their abilities, but on God's. God is not looking to what we can become, but what He can become through us. He desires for us to see ourselves becoming a channel of present blessing rather than a reservoir of past memories. Paul wrote to the Corinthians these words;

> *"Brothers, think of what you were when you were called. Not many of you were wise by human standards; not many were influential; not many were of noble birth. But God chose the foolish things of the world to shame the wise; God chose the weak things of the world to shame the strong. He chose the lowly things of this world and the despised things-- and the things that are not-- to nullify the things that are, so that no one may boast before him. It is because of him that you are in Christ Jesus, who has become for us wisdom from God-- that is, our righteousness, holiness and redemption. Therefore, as it is written: "Let him who boasts boast in the Lord."* (1 Corinthians 1:26-31)

The Lord is also looking for ways to show Himself strong on our behalf.

> *"For the eyes of the LORD range throughout the earth to strengthen those whose hearts are fully committed to him."*
> (2 Chronicles 16:9)

The Lord desires to put His work on display in our lives.

> *"As he went along, he saw a man blind from birth. His disciples asked him, "Rabbi, who sinned, this man or his parents, that he was born blind?" "Neither this man nor his parents sinned," said Jesus, "but this happened so that the work of God might be displayed in his life."* (John 9:1-3)

Becoming enables our coming out of the belief that victory is based solely on our abilities. We must remember that any lacking of ability is a relative term. As sons of God we may lack the necessary qualifications or abilities to perform a given act or service, but with God's help,

> *"we can do all things through Christ who strengthens us."*
> (Philippians 4:13)

The Lord understands who we are on our own.

"As a father has compassion on his children, so the LORD has compassion on those who fear him; for he knows how we are formed, he remembers that we are dust." (Psalm 103:13-14)

The Lord remembers what we can do on our own.

"I am the vine; you are the branches. If a man remains in me and I in him, he will bear much fruit; apart from me you can do nothing." (John 15:5)

As sons of God, we are called to trust in the Lord.

"Some trust in chariots and some in horses, but we trust in the name of the LORD our God." (Psalm 20:7)

"Trust in the LORD with all your heart and lean not on your own understanding; in all your ways acknowledge him, and he will make your paths straight. Do not be wise in your own eyes; fear the LORD and shun evil. This will bring health to your body and nourishment to your bones." (Proverbs 3:5-8)

Remember our becoming happens as Christ lives in us.

"I have been crucified with Christ and I no longer live, but Christ lives in me. The life I live in the body, I live by faith in the Son of God, who loved me and gave himself for me." (Galatians 2:20)

Because Christ lives in us, as sons of God we now possess sufficient abilities to understand any issue, problem, or situation; to make a reasonable decision concerning it; and to understand and appreciate the potential consequences of the decision. We are not incompetent, we are...

➢ Redeemed from the curse of the law. (Galatians 3:13)
➢ New creations. The old is gone, the new is come!
  (2 Corinthians 5:17)
➢ More than conquerors through him that loves us.
  (Romans 8:37)
➢ Able to go up and take the country. We can certainly do it.
  (Numbers 13:30)
➢ Qualified to share in the inheritance of the saints.
  (Colossians 1:12)
➢ Victorious through our Lord Jesus Christ.
  (1 Corinthians 15:57)
➢ Pressing toward the goal for which God has called us.
  (Philippians 3:14)
➢ Rejoicing in the Lord at all times. (Philippians 4:4)
➢ Overcoming the world. (1 John 5:5)

As we take our first real steps toward becoming we must guard against every attack on our identity. We must remember of how Moses began by expressing his unbelief in his ability. He compared himself to others, and he felt weak up beside their strengths. Moses felt he lacked the ability because he had not been trained. Moses felt that he was not suitable or possessed the sufficient skill, knowledge or experience to accomplish the call of God on his life.

Moses had experience that he believed was not related to his identity. Moses had been raised in Pharaoh's household. Moses had spent forty years in the wilderness. Moses had been tending sheep. Moses did not have relationship with the Israelite sons.

Based on past performance…Moses was "slow" of speech. The word for "slow" in Hebrew means: dull, boring, uninteresting, stammering. This is similar to Paul's words in 1 Corinthians 2:1. *When I came to you, brothers, I did not come with eloquence or superior wisdom as I proclaimed to you the testimony about God.*

Moses was convinced his lack of ability would hinder his becoming. Moses suggested that God use someone else. God then asked Moses a question that He asked in a similar way to many others in scripture;

"The LORD said to him, "Who gave man his mouth? Who makes him deaf or mute? Who gives him sight or makes him blind? Is it not I, the LORD?" (Exodus 4:11)

"Do you have an arm like God's, and can your voice thunder like his?" (Job 40:9)

"To whom will you compare me? Or who is my equal?" says the Holy One. Lift your eyes and look to the heavens: Who created all these? He who brings out the starry host one by one, and calls them each by name. Because of his great power and mighty strength, not one of them is missing." (Isaiah 40:25-26)

From our becoming…*we will see*. We will see God on the throne of heaven and the throne of our heart. We will see Christ in the creation and in the sons who surround us as His Cloud of witnesses. We will see that no matter how dark the night, joy comes in the morning. The more we see, the more sight we have, as we continue becoming the sons of God.

Perhaps you are struggling with your identity. Perhaps you don't feel qualified to be the person God is calling you to become. I want you to know that in your becoming a son of God you must not focus on how others feel about your identity or shortcomings.

As I stated earlier false identity generally begins when others. Most of the time others don't know who we really are or who God made us to become. That kind of false identity begins to grow when one allows others to determine our identity for us. The identity of Israel changed when a new king, who did not know about Joseph, came to power in Egypt. (Exodus 1:8) When the Pharaoh of Egypt no longer understood that it was Joseph and the people of Israel that God has used to save Egypt and the known world, he called the Israelites "slave" instead of "brother."

There is an eternal principle at work here.

Whatever you call a thing is what it becomes.

Why? Because you will always treat a thing whatever name you give it. This includes the name you give yourself!

The scripture illustrates this principle when recording the words of the Lord to Abraham and Sarah.

"Neither shall thy name any more be called Abram, but thy name shall be Abraham; for a father of many nations have I made thee. And God said unto Abraham, As for Sarai thy wife, thou shalt not call her name Sarai, but Sarah shall her name be." (Sarah: that is Princess) (Genesis 17:15)

The Lord also applied this principle with Jacob, the grandson of Abraham.

"And he said, Thy name shall be called no more Jacob, but Israel: for as a prince hast thou power with God and with men, and hast prevailed." (Israel: that is, A prince of God) (Genesis 32:28)

But perhaps the most obvious example is Jesus renaming Simon with the name, Peter or Cephas;

"One of the two which heard John speak, and followed him, was Andrew, Simon Peter's brother. He first findeth his own brother Simon, and saith unto him, We have found the Messias, which is, being interpreted, the Christ. And he brought him to Jesus. And when Jesus beheld him, he said, Thou art Simon the son of Jonah: thou shalt be called Cephas, which is by interpretation, A stone." (John 1:40-42)

There was even mistaken identity spoken about the Lord Jesus. One day Jesus asked his disciples about His identity;

"When Jesus came into the coasts of Caesarea Philippi, he asked his disciples, saying, Whom do men say that I the Son of man am? And they said, Some say that thou art John the Baptist: some, Elias; and others, Jeremias, or one of the prophets. He saith unto them, But whom say ye that I am? And Simon Peter answered and said, Thou art the Christ, the Son of the living God." (Matthew 16:13-16)

When we are misnamed and given a false identity, the door is opened for others to mistreat us. The Egyptians began identifying the Israelites with the word "slave" and then began treating them as though they were slaves. Pharaoh put out a decree that he wanted the Israelites lives to be made bitter with hard labor. This hard labor included the making of brick and mortar as well as working in the fields. The Egyptians began using their former saviors as slaves and treating them ruthlessly. (Exodus 1:14)

This created missed identity caused the Egyptians to oppress the purposes of God in the lives of the Israelites. The wrong identity also caused the Israelites to lose the purpose for which they had been given through Abraham. God had given them an identity as Abraham's seed. Theirs was an identity that would bless the whole earth. But slavery, whether real or imagined, established a terrible self image not only for individuals, but in the whole nation of Israel. Like Israel or the Africans brought to America in the 16th and 17th centuries, slavery imposes an identity that causes fear, poverty and great distress which is passed down for generations.

Sin is a hard taskmaster. Humanity became slaves to sin because of Adam's fall. Paul wrote to the Romans that without God every person is a slave to sin. (Romans 6:20) This slavery to sin has created a "slave" mentality not only among those without God, but also many who have come to the saving knowledge of Jesus Christ.

This type of mentality happens when:

➢ One is burdened down with cruel or unjust opinions or restraints.
➢ One is subject to an arduous or harsh exercise of authority or power.
➢ One is "put down" for the purpose of suppressing one's purpose or potential.

False Identity, like the worst narcotic, is habit forming. This is the problem today for criminologists. Paroled or pardoned criminals nearly always go back to crime; many sink again into their former way of life, as the slaves of wrong thinking. But this also has happened in many sons of God. Sin isn't the only culprit. Religion has also enslaved many with an identity of self worthlessness. There are many who have been born of Spirit who remain self loathing. Many sons of God have preached freedom of the spirit while creating bondage for the soul through layers of legalism. (Galatians 5:1)

Jesus Christ came to deliver all humanity not only from the slavery of sin, but from the slave mentality. This deliverance can only begin with a true revelation of who the Lord Jesus is and who we are in Him. He is the God of Abraham, Isaac and Jacob. He is the Christ, the Son of the

Living God. He is the Author and Finisher, the Beginning and the End. The writer of the book of Hebrews declared our focus must be upon the race before us... "Looking unto JESUS THE AUTHOR AND FINISHER OF OUR FAITH!" It was this view of Jesus that continually causes havoc to hell's program. He overthrew thrones and principalities and continues to reign victorious forever and ever!

Jesus Christ is the BE-LOVED Son! As sons of God we are BE-LOVED!

In the Apocalypse John not only saw the Lord Jesus standing, but he also saw us! We are "in Christ." As mature sons (like the Lord Jesus) we have hair white as wool, (a sign of maturity), eyes as a flaming fire, (possessing purity in the window of our soul), around our middle a golden band, (the belt of truth tried in the fire) and feet of brazen brass, (a holy mixture of soul and spirit). The Lord wanted John as well as all sons of God to know that Jesus Christ was the One who was dead, but NOW was alive forever. And as sons, His death is our death and His life is our life! Just as He is the Conqueror of death, hell and the grave, so are we! Hallelujah!

Because of who He is....*we become.* Our identity must not be found in the surname of our family, or the title of our denomination, neither can it be because of a position in business or ministry. In our becoming sons of God the truth of who we really are has been deposited by the Holy Spirit into our hearts and minds.

Jesus said,

"Whoever lives by the truth comes into the light." (John 3:21)

And that

"if one hold's to His teaching, that same person knows the truth, and the truth will set us free." (John 8:31-32)

Paul also told the Philippians

"that whatever is true...think about such things."

(Philippians 4:8)

The truth concerning our Identity is established as we submit to THE Truth.

➢ We died with Christ and anyone who has died is FREE!

"For we know that our old self was crucified with him so that the body of sin might be done away with, that we should no longer be slaves to sin because anyone who has died has been freed from sin." (Romans 6:6,7)

➢ Christ lives within us and anyone who is alive in Christ is FREE!

"I have been crucified with Christ and I no longer live, but Christ lives in me. The life I live in the body, I live by faith in the Son of God, who loved me and gave himself for me." (Galatians 2:20)

➢ The Holy Spirit Lives within us and where He is there is FREEDOM!
"Now the Lord is the Spirit, and where the Spirit of the Lord is, there is freedom." (2 Corinthians 3:17)

➢ We come out of the false when we CHOOSE TO BE Our True Identity.
"But now, this is what the LORD says-- he who created you, O Jacob, he who formed you, O Israel: "Fear not, for I have redeemed you; I have summoned you by name; you are mine. When you pass through the waters, I will be with you; and when you pass through the rivers, they will not sweep over you. When you walk through the fire, you will not be burned; the flames will not set you ablaze. Do not be afraid, for I am with you." (Isaiah 43:1-2; 5)

How precious and dear to the heart of God are His sons! That which Ezekiel saw in his vision was the very genesis of sonship as from the fire, the brightness, and the whirlwind the Son of God came forth. And so delighted was the Father in that Son that He proclaimed the edict, *"Let Us make man in Our image and after Our likeness, and let Us give him dominion."* So this Son of God from eternity became the Son of man, and, as I stated earlier, the Father proclaimed Him to be at the river Jordan as "My BE-LOVED Son." Jesus became the Captain and has led the way whereby we who were the sons of men could be proclaimed SONS BE-LOVED BY GOD!

All who have the first fruits of the Spirit groan within themselves while we wait for the completion in Him. We have received the Spirit of adoption. Therefore our spirits loudly cry, *"Abba, Father."*

"The Spirit Himself beareth witness with our spirit that we are the children (teknon) of God; and if children, then heirs; heirs of God, and joint heirs with Christ if so be that we suffer with Him, that we may be also glorified together." (Romans 8:17)

I want you to make this decree,

Abba, Father! I am your son! My identity is found in you. Cleansing, purifying, changing until I'm fashioned and become just like You. Then in all of Your glorious fullness I shall come. Deep will call to deep, "Abba, Father, I am Your son."

CHAPTER FIVE

Becoming Sons

It is a somewhat paradoxical reality that only sons with maturity ever question their immaturity. True humility is a quality in precious supply within the Church. Yet is the ministry is to rise up into its rightful place at the proper time, God must be given opportunity to sift through the thought and intent of the heart.

The becoming son must allow the sometimes painful process whereby every hope, plan and desire within our lives is tested to see whether they are of God or man. True humility is the key to this process. Humility allows us to be strong in the Lord. Humility allows God to raise us up to our rightful place in ministry. Humility is the philosophical foundation for scriptural sonship.

Becoming a proper son of God requires a willingness to endure the different seasons of the maturation process. It is these seasons that enables us to correctly see within ourselves. Maturity sacrifices the promotion of self and the comfort of position for a posterity that will continue in the vision and the purpose of God.

We must ask these hard questions...

➤ Where am I in the maturation process?
➤ Is it possible that I am only a spiritual adolescent?
➤ Am I truly willing to become what the Lord needs me to be?
➤ Am I a son in right order with a ministry father?
➤ What motivates me? My gifting, my position or my love for God?
➤ Is there a desire to fulfill my purpose and reach my destiny?
➤ Do I have a desire to bring glory to God and victory to others?

➤ Is the life I live bringing honor to my ministry father?

Abraham is a great example of a man with a becoming identity. The Bible says,

"Abraham **will surely become** *a great and powerful nation, and all nations on earth will be blessed through him. For I have chosen him, so that he will direct his children and his household after him to keep the way of the LORD by doing what is right and just, so that the LORD will bring about for Abraham what he has promised him." (Genesis 18:18-19)*

The Lord knew Abraham would perpetuate by faith the pattern of righteousness that the Lord had entrusted to him. Abraham wanted to see the righteousness in his heart come to fruition in the heart of his offspring. (He wanted to be-come the blessing) The Lord has commissioned each son of God to follow in the steps of Abraham (Romans 4), not because of their great oratory, administrative genius or sonship expertise, but because the Lord knows that within each son is the ability to correctly and faithfully impart the spiritual pattern given to them in the subsequent generations that follow.

We see this needed spiritual identity in the story of the prodigal son. Luke 15:20 says,

"But while he was still a long way off, his father saw him and was filled with compassion for him; he ran to his son, threw his arms around him and kissed him."

The prodigal son's father's heart was a giving heart. A father does not give because of what a son can do for him, but rather a father gives because the son is in his heart. A son may leave the presence of the father, but he is still in his father's heart. By being in a father's heart the son sooner or later will have the opportunity to experience real forgiveness. A son learns forgiveness by watching a father for-give. As Mark Hanby said, "Nothing to give. Nothing to offer. The prodigal son sought to become a servant, but the father embraced his grimy body reeking with the stench of the pig pen and hugged him tenaciously so close to his heart that the fragrant anointing of the Spirit exceeded overwhelmed, and displaced the pernicious odor of the past."

The father's view of his son was not contingent upon the son's behavior; it was grounded in steadfast love. The father's view of his son was not based upon the memory of old hurts, but upon ongoing commitment. He passed the identity he chose for his son to be imparted into his son. How do we know this? The bible says that when the prodigal had reached the bottom of the barrel...he came to himself. In other words, he woke up to the identity his father had given to him. He saw himself not as others saw him but as his father saw him.

Warning, don't get too close. The heart of the Heavenly Father will get a hold of you. The same can be said of a spiritual father who has chosen to become the blessing to the lives of his ministry sons. Such a father will pull you so close that the anointing on his life will wash away and overcome the odor of a rebellious past. A lost identity and a squandered inheritance will be replaced by a hundred fold blessing of glory and grace.

We see the becoming identity in the Apostle Paul and his protégé, Timothy. Paul met Timothy in the city of Lystra. During Paul's second missionary journey Timothy joined Paul's apostolic team. His heart toward Timothy was a caring heart (1 Timothy 1:2); a connected heart (Acts 16:3) and a grateful heart (Philippians 2:19-22).

The life and ministry of Timothy is a wonderful example of a son who was becoming and I believe became all that the Lord desired. Timothy was willing to have removed from his life any habits that kept his life and ministry anemic. There is no doubt in my mind that Timothy struggled with temptations and shortcomings but he refused to allow the enemy to stop God's promises from becoming reality in his life. He evidently watched the example God set before him (Paul) and was willing to embrace the instruction and receive the impartation by the Holy Spirit through Paul.

Timothy had been with Paul when the ministry in Philippi began. Years later Paul sat chained in the dirty Roman prison, the Philippians and Timothy were greatly concerned about his welfare, but his thoughts were on things above. The Roman dictator had put him where he wanted him…in chains. But as far as this life was concerned Caesar could not bind his spirit. Paul had the spirit of an eagle, and his spirit was soaring in the heavenlies of divine revelation. He had chosen years before to become one of God's sons. He had received the spirit of adoption. His identity in Christ had now determined his philosophy of life. He had passed that same identity to his spiritual son in the Lord, Timothy.

From his point of view, the almost unbearable circumstances were only an annoyance. As far as earthly creature comforts were concerned, Paul would not let his situation affect his relationship with Jesus Christ or those he loved. He had been stripped of earthly wealth and possessions, but he was richer by far than any of his captors. Many saw him being chained to the guards, while Paul saw the guards chained to him. Sitting in those chains he wrote:

"Unto me who am less than the least of all saints is this grace given, that I should preach among the Gentiles the UNSEARCH-ABLE RICHES of Christ!" (Ephesians 3:8)

It was while in prison, when Caesar thought he had the voice of this great apostle stilled, that Paul wrote words under the inspiration of the Holy Ghost that would change the identity of millions of sons for thousands of years to come.

I pray that you hear me today! You are a son of God. You are free to become the vision within your heart. You do not have to be in bondage to your circumstances. Such circumstances have been used in the past to establish the foundations of the world's religions. These religions are continually focused on the circumstances. Religion says that either they are for the purpose of our destruction or for the purpose of our edification. But there are no circumstances or any one earthly force that can keep you from becoming God's will for your life. If your current situation is trying to move your focus off of The Lord Jesus and seemingly is trying to bind you, be it your health, finances, a lifeless church, geographical isolation, or any other thing, these things cannot keep you from becoming unless you submit to them.

Paul knew how to relate to his chains in Rome! He had overcome them in Philippi! He and Silas had been beaten, battered and bound into the inner prison. Roman prisons had three sections. The prisoners in the first were kept inside a high wall. It was a place of bondage but natural light. The second section was inside. Lit candles provided the light to eat and see. But in the inner prison or third section there was no light. It was there that heavy darkness prevailed. Known to us as the dungeon or the hole where there is isolation, stench and death.

It appears as though Paul saw the prison in the light of the tabernacle of Moses. In the three rooms that Moses built there was natural light, artificial light and no light. Taught at the feet of Gamaliel, Paul knew that the Lord God dwells in the thick darkness. (Exodus 20:21) In the darkest part of the night he and Silas began to pray and sing praises. Instead of complaint and criticism the sons of God began to declare the mercies of the Lord! They entered with thanksgiving and praise and God came to dwell in their presence. Perhaps they sang from the Psaltery;

Psalm 34:1-6 *"I will bless the LORD at all times: his praise shall continually be in my mouth. My soul shall make her boast in the LORD: the humble shall hear thereof, and be glad. O magnify the LORD with me, and let us exalt his name together. I sought the LORD, and he heard me, and delivered me from all my fears. They looked unto him, and were lightened: and their faces were not* *ashamed. This poor man cried, and the LORD heard him, and saved him out of all his troubles."*

Or;

Psalm 100:1-5 *"Make a joyful noise unto the LORD, all ye lands. Serve the LORD with gladness: come before his presence with singing. Know ye that the LORD he is God: it is he that hath made us, and not we ourselves; we are his people, and the sheep of his pasture. Enter into his gates with thanksgiving, and into his courts with praise: be thankful unto him, and bless his name. For the LORD is good; his mercy is everlasting; and his truth endureth to all generations."*

God then filled the prison where Paul and Silas were held. The earth shook, the doors of the prison were blown open and the chains fell away. Paul's true identity created victory where there appeared defeat. God filled their praises and the enemy was overcome. The glorious light of God filled man's dungeon of darkness.

Timothy knew this story. He had seen the result of Paul's becoming identity. If Paul or Timothy were speaking to us today they would declare…remember, you too are becoming a son of God! You can rise above any situation! Your identity is found in Who He Is! He is the Lord God Almighty and the earth (that's you) is filled with His glory! Lift up your eyes. Lift up your voice. Lift up your hands. The greatest struggle is never the prison, but the false identity imprisonment that our memory uses against us. No weapon formed against us will prosper! This is our heritage. This is our inheritance!

Remember the Apostle John on the Isle of Patmos. He had been banished from society, exiled on a lonely island, left to die, with no possibility of any further ministry. The Apostle probably felt as though all of his opportunities for ministry were behind him, that there was nothing at all he could do as far as the work of the Kingdom of God was concerned. John had no churches to go to, no people to preach to, and no sick to heal. The Roman government had banished him to an island, separated him from the people, but Rome could not chain his spirit. For on the Lord's Day John found himself "in the Spirit." He was called upward to see from heaven's point of view. Like an eagle he soared to heights never before attained.

"And immediately I was in the spirit: and, behold, a throne was set in heaven, and one sat on the throne. The four and twenty elders fall down before him that sat on the throne, and worship him that lives forever and ever, and cast their crowns before the throne, saying, Thou art worthy, O Lord, to receive glory and honor and

power: for thou hast created all things, and for thy pleasure they are and were created." (Revelation 4:2, 10-11)

God has ordered the steps of the righteous. Every day of your life has been written in God's book. (Psalm 139:16) No prison of godless or religious philosophy can hold that one who is committed to their becoming, whose heart is not tied to things of this earth. God is speaking in this hour that before we can "be-coming into our promised inheritance" we must "come out of our previous way of living and thinking." (false identity) Listen to these words spoken to Moses concerning the deliverance of Israel,

"I have promised to bring you up out of your misery..."
(Exodus 3:17)

And,

"And he brought us out from thence, that he might bring us in, to give us the land which he swore unto our fathers."
(Deuteronomy 6:23)

There is nothing that brings more identifiable misery to a son of God than religious Christianity. If we look up the academic definition we find that religion is a system of thought, feeling, and action that is shared by a group of people. This system gives the members an object of devotion; a code of behavior by which individuals may judge the personal and social consequences of their actions; and a frame of reference by which individuals may relate to their group and their universe. Usually, religion concerns itself with that which transcends the known, the natural, or the expected; it is an acknowledgment of, as well as, a philosophical limitation of the extraordinary, the mysterious, and the supernatural.

The problem is that religion has invaded Christianity which has resulted in a false identity. This religious pseudo Christian philosophy seeks to evaluate God and the circumstances of life from mankind's point of view.

The modern church has become man centered, need focused and entertainment based. It is mankind's way of trying to determine, define and describe who God is, (His identity) what God expects from man (our false identity) and what man should expect from God (false hope).

We see this same religious spirit in the Egyptians, Greeks and Romans who worshiped many gods and goddesses, all of which looked like them. All of these kingdoms believed that their king (Pharaoh or Caesar) had descended from the greatest of the gods.

Christianity is the religion that is most adhered to in the western world. The definition that is most widely accepted is that Christianity is a religion centered on the life and teachings of Jesus as presented in the New Testament and based on the God of the Old Testament. The problem is that religious Christianity has given Jesus a false identity. He is portrayed as a poor, itinerate and fool hardy preacher. He has been painted as a soft, sissified and silly son.

Thankfully many well known Christians, believe that Jesus is the only begotten Son of God and the Messiah prophesied in the Hebrew Bible (Old Testament). Yet there is great disagreement about His claims that He, Jesus Christ is God incarnate, a teacher, the model of a virtuous life, the reveler of God, and most importantly the Savior of humanity who suffered, died and was resurrected to bring about salvation from sin. Few really maintain that Jesus ascended into heaven and will one day return to judge the living and the dead, granting everlasting life to his followers.

The problem with the identity this kind of Christianity brings is that:

➤ It sees and describes God from man's perspective.
➤ It establishes the ways of how man can reach God.
➤ It focuses on what men must do to experience God.
➤ It creates a philosophy that is need based.
➤ It declares heaven as the best God can offer and points   toward heaven as the ultimate "religious" experience.
➤ The different "sects" or "denominations" of Christianity declare to have the "correct" view of all that encompasses who God is. This division has produced several "different identities" in the body of Christ.

Religious Christianity can never be the substitute for our possessing the same identity of God's Son. Jesus Christ exposed the religious as only seeing what was presently before them. The religious saw their relationship with God as one between Master and servant not Father and son. Therefore everything issues out of a slave instead of a "son" mentality.

Biblical sonship on the other hand establishes a loving relationship where the son grows up through a process similar to the natural process human beings experience. This process is a result of God speaking a proceeding word. We see a picture of this process in Galatians chapter four. Verse 1 tells us that the heir (and remember that every believer is an heir of God) is "lord of all". (Notice the small letters in the words heir and lord). This means the son is master and ruler of everything God has given to them. But son's rulership only appears when he is fully matured. Until maturity, as long as he is a child, the son is treated as a servant and is under tutors and governors. His life is governed by others or circumstances.

Any parent knows better than to let a small child govern his own life. As humans, we love the child too much for that. At the age of seven a child may want to the keys to the car, but we don't give them to them. It is after that child has "grown up" and reaches a certain level of maturity that he comes into his inheritance. The fullness of the inheritance can only be realized at a "time appointed of the father." This time appointed of the father has to do with the son being able to rule himself.

The philosophical view of modern Christianity has traditionally prevented a person from "growing up" into the head who is Jesus Christ. Again it is because most ministries are man centered, need focused and entertainment based. Such Christianity appeals to the immature. Yet, without the formation of spiritual maturity Paul says that the sons of God remain in bondage under the elements (circumstances or material values) of the world.

Jesus came to redeem us and bring us to full sonship. In Galatians four verse seven Paul wrote: *"Wherefore thou art no more a servant, but a son; and if a son, then an heir of God through Christ."*

God's doesn't want us to live as servants and receive rewards for our labors here on earth. He wants us to have His nature and live His life. He desires to see maturity in us to the extent that in our becoming, we bear His image, do His will because we have His mind, and share in His inheritance. This inheritance is available because of the "adoption of sons." (Verse 5) The word adoption used here does not have the meaning that we usually apply to it in adopting someone else's child. It is the Greek word: *"huiothesia"*, meaning the "placing as a son". It means for a man to take his own child who has grown from babyhood, through childhood, to a mature manhood, and officially setting him in as a partner with the father in his business and possessions.

The Apostle John tells us in Revelation 21:7 that,

"He that overcometh shall INHERIT all things, and I will be his God, and he shall be MY SON."

This is the philosophy of becoming a son, to inherit all things. And to inherit all things we must continue *BECOMING* God's son. It was necessary that Jesus die, in order to make His will and inheritance effective for us. (Hebrews 9:16). The philosophy of inheritance requires a son to enter and stay in the process of maturity. The maturity of God's sons establishes His inheritance for the generations to come.

"Know therefore that the LORD thy God, he is God, the faithful God, which keepeth covenant and mercy with them that love him and keep his commandments to a thousand generations;" (Deuteronomy 7:9)

The inheritance of sons is realized when everything we are and do is based upon our true identity in Christ Jesus. This identity can only be found in the Scriptures, when we choose to see things from the perspective of the Son and Eternal Word of God. Levels of maturity are revealed in many different ways and in many different scriptures;

John 8:22-30 there are: Seekers, Believers and Disciples who are...
Curious, Concerned or Committed.

In 1 John 2:12-13 there are: Little children, Young men and Fathers who eat...
The Milk, Bread or Meat of the Word.

In Colossians 2:7 sons are: Rooted, Built up and Established...living the Kingdom...in righteousness, peace and joy in the Holy Spirit.

In 2 Corinthians 9:7 givers give: Grudgingly, Out of Necessity and Cheerfully... which produces a harvest of Thirty, Sixty or a Hundred-fold. (Matthew 13:23)

Our inheritance includes a generational vision; that is; the House of the Lord, the local church, is central to the community of God's sons, just as the tribes of Israel were camped around the Mosaic Tabernacle (Num. 2:1-16). The mature sons that are within the local church should oversee the families that constitute the biblical inheritance. Through the relationships of fathers and sons our true identity in Christ must be handed down through many generations (Isaiah 58:12). In every son's home, it should be taught that the House of the Lord is central to our lives. God's sons should love the House and people of God. From a changed heart within, not legal obligation, God's sons should joyfully support the House of the Lord with their time (attendance), their talents (joints of supply), and their treasures (His tithe and our offerings).

Yet there is more than supporting the house of the Lord. We must see ourselves becoming the house of the Lord. We are living and lively stones which are built and established on the reforming ministries of the apostles and prophets. We are being "built up" through love and becoming the house, the dwelling place, the habitation of the Lord. We who were not a people are now the people of God.

The son's "becoming" is inclusive of all of our horizontal relationships in the home and local church and they must be governed by the principles of covenant community. No one lives to themselves (Romans 14:7). And as various parts of His body the sons of God are members one of another and are therefore responsible for one another. Sons should absolutely refuse to lift a hand or raise a word against another brother or sister, knowing that any kind of speech that injures is slanderous, and we will be judged for every idle word by the Lord Himself (Matthew 12:36).

The son's identity should include the Kingdom of God as a present reality and that same Kingdom will expand until the knowledge of His Lordship covers the Earth as the waters cover the sea. The Government of God, including the five-fold ministry, must be established to help God's sons accomplish their purpose in the earth. The Church, universal and local, mystical and tangible, invisible and visible, is the instrument through which that purpose is to be realized.

This biblical view of sonship believes in theocratic (God-ruled) local church government and biblical order (elders, deacons, and saints). Such divine order sets forth a singularity of headship and a plurality of sonship. This order sees God continuing to give us a set man (Senior Pastor) with a distinctive anointing to father the flock of God.

It is in this "becoming" that sons are able to see that who they are in Christ is more important that what they do. Sons of God must grow and serve with passion from His nature within, not a legal obligation, but from a love for God and His people!

The fruit of His divine nature is more important than any charismatic gifting. The purpose of God is to transform His sons to the image and likeness of the Lord Jesus Christ and the high calling of God. It is time to become a people just like Jesus, brothers of whom He is not ashamed.

CHAPTER SIX

Managing Your Becoming

Becoming should not be seen as cost. It's an investment. It really doesn't matter what we pay for making an investment in our lives and ministries. The thing that is relevant is what we get in return. One of the best ways to jeopardize our future in today's world and increase the probability of troubled times is to refuse to learn today what we will need to be productive in the future.

To manage the life that becomes a son of God we must address the daily steps that enable us to endure what I call the three "T's" of trouble, trial and torment. Jesus said in John 10:10; "The thief comes only to steal and kill and destroy: I am come that you might have life and that to the full."

I want you to take special note to not only the words, but the order in which Jesus spoke them. Stealing is the purpose of the thief, but the thief will always escalate to killing and destroying if necessary just like the modern outlaw or gangster. The word steal comes from the Greek word, *klepto*. This is where we get the word, kleptomaniac. A kleptomaniac is an individual that cannot stop stealing. He steals when there is no need or purpose. He steals for the thrill of stealing. Such is the enemy. While most believe Jesus is describing the devil, I want you to also see that the enemy is anything that stands in the way of your becoming.

The Greek word, *thuo,* is translated kill. This type of killing means to sacrifice others for the sake of one's self. It is not the defense of self, others or property. It is killing with selfishness. Which is exactly what selfishness is; it is a killer of the desire to become a blessing to others. And finally the word destroy comes from the Greek word, *apollumi.* The application of this word points toward devastation to the point of obliteration.

I believe there are three giants that must be overcome if we are going to manage the becoming life. These giants seek to bring distress for the purpose of occupying our:

> ➢ Time
> ➢ Mind
> ➢ Money
> ➢ Ministry

The first of these giants is…TROUBLE. Job said, *"I have no peace, no quietness; I have no rest, but only trouble."* (Job 3:26)

Trouble can be defined as the uncontrollable circumstances, the unmet expectations and the personal afflictions that happen in life. Trouble comes in many forms. It can manifest in the circumstances surrounding individual sickness, poverty, or perverted justice. This giant can be even larger and more difficult to deal with. It can include national calamities like the recent earthquake that devastated the island nation of Haiti. It is hard not to feel sadness for those who have lost their lives or been affected by the earthquake. Hitting a massive 7.0 on the Richter scale the earthquake and resulting devastation has left approximately 700,000 people dead and millions hurting and homeless. These numbers are simply overwhelming. Trouble of this sort will leave the country in a state of recovery for many, many years. No doubt the money required for repairs and for aid will be just as staggering as the death toll.

Trouble can also come in the form of spiritual persecution.

Matthew 13:20-21 says,

> *"The one who received the seed that fell on rocky places is the man who hears the word and at once receives it with joy. But since he has no root, he lasts only a short time. When trouble or persecution comes because of the word, he quickly falls away."*

The trouble comes as a result of the Word of God or new understanding about the Word being planted into our lives. Many times after we have received a new revelation we find ourselves dealing with the very circumstances that either confirm or disprove what we have come to know. Jesus said that those who are shallow (immature) in their understanding are many times "offended" when this type of trouble comes. In other words, most immature sons fail to understand that for the Word to be effectual their lives it must be tested and tried. The Greek word used in this context is *tarasso*. It means to agitate, to disturb, to cause one inward commotion or turmoil, therefore taking away peace of mind, making one restless, anxious, perplexed or distressed.

While recognizing that trouble is part of this life the Bible has declared that no matter how devastating the circumstances the Lord will never leave us or forsake us. The Psalms are full of comforting and encouraging words concerning the problems and difficulties in life:

Psalm 9:9 says,

"The LORD is a refuge for the oppressed, a stronghold in times of trouble."

Psalm 32:7;

"You are my hiding place; you will protect me from trouble and surround me with songs of deliverance."

Psalm 41:1;

"Blessed is he who has regard for the weak; the LORD delivers him in times of trouble."

Psalm 46:1;

"God is our refuge and strength, an ever-present help in trouble."

And finally, Psalm 138:7;

"Though I walk in the midst of trouble, you preserve my life; you stretch out your hand against the anger of my foes, with your right hand you save me."

One of my favorite passages comes from a Psalm David wrote. We see his heart hurting but filled with confidence in the Lord.

Psalm 27:4-5,

"One thing I ask of the LORD, this is what I seek: that I may dwell in the house of the LORD all the days of my life, to gaze upon the beauty of the LORD and to seek him in his temple. For in the day of trouble he will keep me safe in his dwelling; he will hide me in the shelter of his tabernacle and set me high upon a rock."

What are the steps needed to overcome the giant of trouble? We first must again see ourselves living the life of the Son of God (Galatians 2:20). Then we must embrace the truth that even Jesus expected trouble. Yet He didn't run from it. He faced it head on. He told His disciples, *"I have told you these things, so that in me you may have peace. In this world you will have trouble. But take heart! I have overcome the world."* (John 16:33)

Overcoming trouble begins with thanksgiving. The Apostle Paul who knew the giant of trouble well told the Philippians, *Do not be anxious about anything, but in everything, by prayer and petition, with thanksgiving, present your requests to God.* His insight tells us that we should be open and honest before the Lord. We should pour out our complaints before him, and share with the Lord the trouble we are in. (Psalm 142:2)

Next, we should seek encouragement first from the words of the Lord Himself. He spoke to Joshua who was facing the situation of a former son's passing (Moses) and the difficulty in leading the nation of Israel into the Promised Land. The Lord told Joshua,

> *"Be strong and courageous. Do not be terrified; do not be discouraged, for the LORD your God will be with you wherever you go."* (Joshua 1:9)

Then we should encourage ourselves by retelling and replaying the victories God has previously given. We see this principle in the situation where the Philistines and specifically the giant called Goliath were "troubling" Israel. The ensuing battle between an Israelite shepherd boy by the name of David and the giant has been used as an example of overcoming trouble for thousands of years. There are several ideals David held to that enabled him to overcome his enemy and bring victory to God's people.

First of all, David knew it was what was on the inside of a man that mattered.

> *"The LORD does not look at the things man looks at. Man looks at the outward appearance, but the LORD looks at the heart."* (1 Samuel 16:7)

Also, David was willing to be faithful in small things.

> *"Early in the morning David left the flock with a shepherd, loaded up and set out, as Jesse had directed."* (1 Samuel 17:20)

Third, David recognized that old armor and weapons wouldn't work.

> *"'I cannot go in these,' he said to Saul, 'because I am not used to them." So he took them off."* (1 Samuel 17:39)

David then fought not with natural weaponry. He chose to face Goliath with powerful spiritual weapons.

> *"David said to the Philistine, 'You come against me with sword and spear and javelin, but I come against you in the name of the LORD Almighty,'"* (1 Samuel 17:45)

Finally, David faced his giant...face to face.

> *"As the Philistine moved closer to attack him, David ran quickly toward the battle line to meet him."* (1 Samuel 17:48)

There are several things to learn from David's victory. First he encouraged himself when others criticized him. Just before the battle David's older brother tried to speak doubt, fear and unbelief into David's heart. But rejecting it David then declared to the King that he had killed both the lion and the bear (1 Samuel 17:36) with his bare hands. He used the positive experience of the past to build upon. David knew that he had overcome similar trouble before and he believed that he and God could do it again.

There was a song many years ago that stated...He'll do it again. The lyrics go like this;

You may feel down and feel like God has somehow forgotten
That are faced with circumstances that you can't get through
Right now it seems that there's no way out You're going under
God's proven time and time again He'll take care of you
Chorus
He'll do it again (God will do it again)...He'll do it again (Yes He
will do it again)
Just take a look at where you are now; And where you have been
Has He always come through for you, He's the same now as then
(Don't you know God has not changed)
You may not know how You may not know when...But He'll do it
again

David used this same technique in 1 Samuel 30 when he and his men returned to Ziklag to find the enemy had ravaged their camp and had taken most of the women and children hostage. The Bible says that David and his men wept aloud until they had no strength left to weep. In fact, David's two wives had been captured-- Ahinoam of Jezreel and Abigail, the widow of Nabal of Carmel. David was greatly distressed because the men were talking of stoning him; each one was bitter in spirit because of his sons and daughters had been taken. But David encouraged himself in the LORD his God.

I want to encourage you that as you become all God desires that when difficulties and troubles arise remember that the victory is already won. The Lord Jesus has spoiled whatever enemies you face. Like Paul in 2 Corinthians 1:3-5, I encourage you to offer thanksgiving and praise to the God and Father of our Lord Jesus Christ. He is a Father of compassion. He is the God of all comfort. He will comfort, strengthen and provide for you in all your troubles. Then, you will be able to comfort those around you in any trouble with the comfort you have received from God. For just as the sufferings of Christ flow over into our lives, so also through Christ our comfort overflows.

What comfort is the Apostle talking about?

First of all, we are never alone. The Father of compassion brings and bestows goodness and mercy in time of need. (Psalm 23:6) He gives consolation and companionship when others leave or forsake us.

(2 Thessalonians 2:16) Our Lord and God delivers (Psalm 34:17) and rescues (Jeremiah 20:13).

As sons of God, who are becoming and maturing, our experiences will enable us to comfort others. Blessing others brings blessing to our lives. Dealing correctly with trouble qualifies us to minister to others. Because personal experience coupled with God's Word and anointing is the avenue of effective ministry. We can then say like Paul,

"We are troubled on every side, yet not distressed; we are perplexed, but not in despair; Persecuted, but not forsaken; cast down, but not destroyed." (2 Corinthians 4:8-9)

The second giant is...TEMPTATION. Like Trouble, Temptation tries to bring distress for the purpose of occupying our: Time... Mind... Money... Ministry.

"Jesus was led by the Spirit into the desert to be tempted by the devil." (Matthew 4:1)

Temptation is anything aimed at the desire of our will. Temptation can be seen in the illustration of a fish being enticed to leave its place of provision and protection. When our soul yields to or grasps temptation, sin is conceived. Therefore, sin is the union of our mind, will, or emotions with the temptation. The result is conception, formation and delivery. (Like a human life) Sin is like digging a hole and then falling into it. Sin returns (like a boomerang) to steal, kill and destroy the one who employed it.

The Apostle Paul tells us, like trouble there are times of when every son of God faces temptation. But we must remember that it is not uncommon to face any kind or form of temptation. He wrote,

"No temptation has seized you except what is common to man. And God is faithful; he will not let you be tempted beyond what you can bear. But when you are tempted, he will also provide a way out so that you can stand up under it." (1 Corinthians 10:13)

The Scripture describes temptation in the word: *peirasmo. Peirasmo* means the trial or testing of one's devotion, integrity, virtue, or consistency through adversity, affliction, pleasure or trouble causing an enticement to sin whether arising from inward desires or from outward circumstances. Temptation therefore in the Scripture sense has possibilities of holiness as well as of sin. For as all experience tells us, it is one thing to be tempted, it is another thing to fall. When tempted--one may rejoice in it (James 1:2), since in temptation, by conquering it, one may achieve a higher and nobler life.

"With every temptation always comes a way of escape."
(1 Corinthians 10:13b)

The way of escape (Greek: *tên ekbasin*), means that "the way out" is always there right along with the temptation. We must remember it is not our reborn spirit that is being tempted. Our spirit is God's spirit. He is living His life through us. Therefore we must recognize it is the flesh and then the soul that is tempted.

"The spirit is willing, but the flesh is weak." (Matthew 26:41)

And

"The carnal mind (the soul ruled by the flesh) is hostile to God.
It does not submit to God's law, nor can it do so." (Romans 8:7)

While weakness of the flesh and soul may yield to temptation and become distrustful of God the "way out" is always "by the spirit." (Zechariah 4:6) Jesus teaches that when we are tempted the doorway of escape opens through prayer.

"And lead us not into temptation, but deliver us from evil." (Matthew 6:13)

"Watch and pray so that you will not fall into temptation." (Matthew 26:41)

The Lord Jesus Christ is our example when it comes to how a son of God should overcome temptation. In Luke 4:1-13 the writer shares the story of Jesus being tempted by the devil. Each of these temptations remember is "common to man."

The first temptation began at the end of a forty day fast where Jesus had eaten nothing. The bible says that afterward "He was hungry." The devil appeared at that moment to tempt Jesus. He used the desire of the flesh for the basis of setting his first trap. He told Jesus that He should turn the stones into bread or in other words, to use supernatural power (i.e., the anointing) to bless Himself. Satan was trying to get Jesus to be "self-ish." This is foundational essence of man's original fall. The serpent beguiled Adam and Eve by getting them to focus on what they wanted and desired. This is why I have spoken so directly about the modern Church being so man centered, need focused and entertainment based. I am convinced that the Lord's Church has fallen for being "self-ish".

This is where we must ask the Lord to give us understanding from John 8:25-32,

"Then said THEY unto Him, 'WHO ART THOU?' And JESUS saith unto them, 'Even the same that I said unto you from the beginning. I have many things to say and to judge of you: but He that sent Me is true; and I speak to the world those things which I have heard of Him.' THEY UNDERSTOOD NOT that He spake to them of the Father. Then said Jesus unto them, 'When ye have LIFTED UP the Son of man,'"

(John 12:32; 19:30) '"then shall ye KNOW that I am He, and that I do nothing of Myself; but as My Father hath taught Me, I speak these things. And He that sent Me is with me: the Father hath not left Me alone; for I do always those things that please Him.' As He spake these words, MANY (the 2nd group) BELIEVED ON HIM.' 'Then said Jesus to those Jews which believed on Him, If ye CONTINUE IN MY WORD, then are YE (the 3rd group) MY DISCIPLES INDEED; And YE shall KNOW the TRUTH'"

(Jn. 14:6), "and the One who is the TRUTH shall MAKE YOU FREE" to (only the 3rd group).

The temptation of the first group is to be ever seeking, listening and learning. They are always seeking and being amazed by the slightest miracles or demonstration of the Spirit. These becoming sons must learn to stay when more mature sons disagree with their way of thinking. They must overcome the temptation to live double-minded lives that are marked by a life of deciding and determining what is going on—ever inquiring—

"Is Jesus (and those whom Jesus sends) FROM GOD OR NOT?" For without victory over this temptation these sons begin to embrace their "mess" and are constantly focused inwardly on what God can do for them.

From this passage we can see that the second group of sons becomes convinced, persuaded, and assured, that Jesus Christ is from God. While they have begun to move forward in their Kingdom understanding they must also be watchful of believing that their church is "the only church" or that their theology is the "only and right theology." It is evident God has opened their eyes and ears, and has spoken to their hearts. We know this because they have admitted and confessed—"Jesus (and those whom Jesus sends) has come to establish the Kingdom of God in their lives!" These love the "message."

We can also see a third group. These are the committed, devoted and faithful. These sons have overcome temptation repeatedly. They have bowed not only their knee but their will as well. These powerfully declare, "There is nothing that I will not do, or give up in the Name of Jesus if He speaks to me. I will do the Father's will." The temptation is to think that the knowledge of a thing (i.e., the Kingdom) is the possession of it. They must overcome the temptation to become like the Gnostics who came to believe that knowledge was more important than ministry.

The second enticement faced by Jesus was the temptation to leap off the temple. This is the lure to become a spiritual fanatic, refusing to be led in paths of holy sanity and heavenly wisdom, and to place God in a position where He had to rescue His Son. This temptation leads to the sin of presumption. The devil understands that distorted truth is not truth. If he can lead a person to presume upon the scriptures and twist them for the purpose of either accomplishing carnal desires or attracting the applause of men, he is successful.

I believe this temptation can best be seen in today's church by viewing most Christian television broadcasts. I have personally been with some of the most famous television preachers and teachers. Sadly, many have fallen to the idea that to continue attracting new listeners and supporters the "show must go on." In other words, the temptation is to make every program better, greater, grander and more exciting than the one before. We almost never see a television preacher have a bad day or preach a not so good message. Why? Because to do so would give the impression that the star of the program is a real person.

For years I have been convinced that this has brought much damage to the Church. Many believers in America now compare their local church and pastor with the super church and star pastor they see every week on television. Because of the nature of television real life is never portrayed. The church program seldom tells that their star is tired, ill or discouraged. He or she is always declaring that all one must do is to believe in God and in their message for everything to turn out alright.

The devil has used this to cause millions around the world to presume that whatever God has spoken to someone else, He has spoken to all of us. An example is the story of a group of young men who spent many days "trying" to walk on water. They had taken the words spoken to Peter by Jesus and had presumed that "if Jesus said it to Peter, then He said it to us." You know the end of the story. None of them could get more than a step and a half before they sank. They then came to the conclusion that they didn't have enough faith. So they spent time in prayer and fasting, but the results were the same. They changed their confession and declared that they would not sink and that they would walk on water, but again the same result. Finally, discouraged they quit. They then used their experience to establish a theology that said God has stopped doing miracles.

We must remember as becoming sons that faith comes by hearing and for there to be hearing, God has to speak. We cannot presume that what He has said to another son is what He is saying to us. We must seek the Lord and ask Him what He desires for us to be and do. Jesus knew the miracles of the Old Testament. He knew the stories of parting the Red Sea, Elijah multiplying the meal and oil, and the three Hebrews surviving the fiery furnace. But He did not hear His Father say…Go to the pinnacle of the temple and jump off. He did not hear the Father declare that such a spectacle would give Jesus a better platform for ministry. He spoke what His Father said and did what He saw His Father do. (John 8)

The third Jesus faced was the temptation to gain authority and power while avoiding difficulty and pain. While the first temptation was to remove hunger; and the second, was to apply presumption, the third, tried to get Jesus to attain authority without sacrifice. This is a temptation aimed specifically at immature sonship.

The Bible says that the devil took Jesus to a high mountain. He showed Jesus the kingdoms of this world. He then tried to convince the Lord to take the shortcut and avoid the cross. The cross represents the cost that must be paid to be an excellent son. Why? Like Thomas looking for the marks of the cross in the body of Jesus, people are looking for authenticity. They want to know that a son has gone before them and has proven their willingness to pay the cost of process.

The devil tried to get Jesus to avoid the process and become a son of the known world just by bowing down and submitting His will. Jesus saw right through the temptation. He knew that without the process there would be lives not touched, experiences not lived and solutions not found. Jesus also knew that this was the very temptation that Adam had fallen to.

The Lord Jesus is our example for overcoming all temptation. Hebrews 4:14-15 says,

> *"Seeing then that we have a great high priest, that is passed into the heavens, Jesus the Son of God, let us hold fast our profession. For we have not an high priest which cannot be touched with the feeling of our infirmities; but was in all points tempted like as we are, yet without sin."*

To be effective when dealing with temptation a son of God must count themselves dead to sin and alive to God in Christ Jesus. (Romans 6:11). A son must keep their eyes focused on Jesus the source and goal of their faith. (Hebrews 12:1-2) Also when we keep our eyes focused upward we are continually reminded that our help comes from the Lord. (Psalm 121:1-2) Being dead sets one free from sin and being alive in Christ Jesus creates a mindset of righteousness. (Romans 6:18; 8:6) This righteous mindset is best seen in 1 Peter 2:9-11;

> *"But you are a chosen people, a royal priesthood, a holy nation, a people belonging to God, that you may declare the praises of him who called you out of darkness into his wonderful light. Once you*

were not a people, but now you are the people of God; once you had
not received mercy, but now you have received mercy. Dear friends,
I urge you, as aliens and strangers in the world, to abstain from
sinful desires, which war against your soul."

The giants of trouble and temptation lose their power with thanksgiving and transformed thinking.

The third giant is torment. Torment causes great physical or mental pain, suffering, or harassment. To be tormented is to be afflicted or harassed by continual repetition of irritations or annoyances: it can also mean to afflict with acute and protracted suffering.

Torment is anything that harasses us to the point of our being weakened to the point that we begin wavering in our commitment to Christ. It can also happen when we become worried to the point of being worn out mentally and physically. Finally, many are tormented because they have been wounded to the point of spiritual trauma and paralysis.

The Apostle Paul shared concerning his torment in his second letter to the Corinthians;

"To keep me from becoming conceited because of these
surpassingly great revelations, there was given me a thorn in my
flesh, a messenger of Satan, to torment me." (2 Corinthians 12:7)

The first cause of torment is fear. 1 John 4:18 says,

"There is no fear in love; but perfect love casteth out fear:
because fear hath torment. He that feareth is not made perfect in
love."

This scripture tells us that fear (phobos) is the opposite of boldness (parresia) and peace (eirene). Fear is a feeling of agitation and anxiety caused by the presence or imminence of real or imagined danger.

Torment can also be caused by unclean or evil spirits. Luke wrote about this in the early ministry of the apostles in the book of Acts 5:16.

"Crowds gathered also from the towns around Jerusalem,
bringing their sick and those tormented by evil spirits, and all of
them were healed."

These spirits belong to the unseen world; they are incapable of manifestation except in the disorders which they cause. Unclean or evil spirits cause a specific type of disturbance, physical or mental, distinguishable not so much by its symptoms which were often of the most general character, as by the torments caused within the mind. Evil spirits can manifest through a thorn in the flesh (2 Corinthians 12:7) or out of the lawlessness of others (2 Peter 2:7-8). Examples of such thorns and lawlessness are: Abortion, Racism, Politically Caused Famine, and Immorality.

Torment can also flow out of the unclean memory of events, abuses or sins in our past. David said,

"My guilt has overwhelmed me like a burden too heavy to bear."
(Psalm 38:4)

And

"For I know my transgressions, and my sin is always before me."
(Psalm 51:3)

How can we effectively overcome torment? First, find a church where there is mature and unconditional love. It is important that if you are being tormented that you make such a place your dwelling place. Also, it is the right place to learn how to love the Lord, youself and others correctly. In such a place the Holy Spirit will help you to become accountable to without becoming offended.

"Love always protects, always trusts, always hopes, always
perseveres. Love never fails." (1 Corinthians 13:7-8a)

Secondly, a son must seek God's great and complete grace. Like temptation and a way of escape cannot be separated… torment and the grace to overcome are as coupled together as well. The power to overcome is continually increased as the torment grows. Paul wrote to the church in Corinth;

"And God is able to make all grace abound to you, so that in
all things at all times, having all that you need, you will abound in
every good work." (2 Corinthians 9:8)

It is also important for a son to abide in the Spirit of glory and of God.

"But rejoice that you participate in the sufferings of Christ, so
that you may be overjoyed when his glory is revealed. If you are
insulted because of the name of Christ, you are blessed, for the
Spirit of glory and of God rests on you. If you suffer, it should not
be as a murderer or thief or any other kind of criminal, or even as
a meddler. However, if you suffer as a Christian, do not be
ashamed, but praise God that you bear that name."
(1 Peter 4:12b-16)

Finally, overcoming trouble, temptation and torment happens as we believe and see our Lord and God as our sun and shield. He will withhold no good thing from those who walk uprightly. Filling our mouths, minds and hearts with praise reminds us of where God has brought us from. He has forgiven our sin and healed our diseases. He sent His Word into our lives and healed them.

CHAPTER SEVEN

Overcoming An Orphan Spirit

One who climbs a mountain for the first time needs to follow a known route; and he needs to have with him, as companion and guide, someone who has been up before and is familiar with the way. To serve as such a companion and guide is precisely the role of the "abba" or spiritual father---whom the Greeks call "geron" and the Russians "starets", a title which in both languages means "papa" or "father." Such an individual is essentially an apostolic or prophetic figure, qualified for the special task of imparting into the lives of others by the Holy Spirit. He is set apart for a special purpose by the hand of God. He is the expression of God Himself for the purpose of making a deposit of the Spirit in the life of another. Why do we need spiritual fathers? Spiritual fathers help develop and disciple God's people bringing an end to the "orphan spirit" that is running rampant in today's church.

God's original plan for man and ministry was to establish a family of spiritual sons (relationship not religion), to establish a priesthood of spiritual son-kings (Dominion not Denomination), and for that priesthood (Ministry) to flow out of sonship (Maturity).

It is relationship that produces sons, while religion produces spiritual orphans. In the natural the children from fatherless homes suffer a startling array of consequences, such as, they are:

➢ 20 times more likely to have behavioral disorders
➢ 9 times more likely to drop out of high school
➢ 10 times more likely to abuse drugs
➢ 20 times more likely to end up in jail or prison

➢ 14 times more likely to be sexually active
➢ 32 times more likely to run away from home
➢ 5 times more likely to commit suicide

To some people, then, the idea of God as "Father" is barren. But Jesus revealed God as a father, who loves, guides, protects, supports, sustains and encourages. God is gentle and strong, patient and just. He gives birth, nurses and carries, waits and explains, sends and welcomes back, forgives and heals.

Along with natural fathers there are many instances in scripture where God gave His sons spiritual fathers. Though these spiritual fathers will never and are not called to take the place of one's natural father, a spiritual father represents the Heavenly Father and all the best He has to give to us. Examples of such father/son relationships are; Moses and Joshua, Jonathan and David, Elijah and Elisha, Paul and Timothy.

A spiritual father is about relationship. A true spiritual father understands that to represent The Heavenly Father requires three things: being there, being aware, and being real. Being there, wanting to be there, committing oneself to being there, being proud of being there, putting up with the messes and the disappointments and shortcomings, and still choosing to be there for a son God has placed in your heart is what fathering is all about.

Every spiritual son needs a relationship with a father. Why? First, a son needs to know that he is never alone. He needs to know that he has a safe and secure place within his father's heart. A true spiritual father and son relationship goes far beyond the term "mentoring." A spiritual father cares for his spiritual sons as his very own natural children.

A son that carries an orphan spirit has relationship with a religion. He is one who feels alone; one who feels that he does not have a safe and secure place where a father can affirm, protect, provide and express God's love to him. He feels as if he doesn't belong unless he surrenders to the pressure of the religious system. He is full of fear, anxiety and insecurity.

The orphan spirit is overcome when righteous fathers through relationship produce righteous sons. These spiritual fathers raise and empower their sons to becoming true sons of God.

Examples of this are:
➢ The Heavenly Father and the Lord Jesus Christ.
  "If you have seen me you have seen The Father." (John 14:9)
  "Then Jesus came to them and said, 'All authority in heaven and on earth has been given to me.'" (Matthew 28:18)
➢ Moses and Joshua

"Now Joshua son of Nun was filled with the spirit of wisdom because Moses had laid his hands on him." (Deuteronomy 34:9)

"But commission Joshua, and encourage and strengthen him, for he will lead this people across and will cause them to inherit the land that you will see." (Deut. 3:28)

➢ Elijah and Elisha

"When they had crossed, Elijah said to Elisha, "Tell me, what can I do for you before I am taken from you?" "Let me inherit a double portion of your spirit," Elisha replied. "You have asked a difficult thing," Elijah said, "yet if you see me when I am taken from you, it will be yours—Elijah went up by a whirlwind into heaven. And Elisha saw it, and he cried, My father, my father, the chariot of Israel, and the horsemen thereof." **(**2 Kings 2: 9-12)

➢ Paul and Timothy

"I hope in the Lord Jesus to send Timothy to you soon, that I also may be cheered when I receive news about you. I have no one else (son) like him," (Ph. 2:19-20a)

"For this reason I remind you to fan into flame the gift of God, which is in you through the laying on of my hands." (2 Timothy 1:6)

Religious systems, denominations and immature pastors produce the orphan spirit and have spiritually impotent sons. These folks may be people who love the Lord, but they are almost always unable to become mature or reproduce spiritual maturity in the lives of others. Most are stuck in the elementary teachings listed in Hebrews 6:1-3. Their theological rejection of spiritual fathers also creates the immaturity described in Ephesians 4:14:

"Then we will no longer be infants, tossed back and forth by the waves, and blown here and there by every wind of teaching and by the cunning and craftiness of men in their deceitful scheming."

The ultimate result of the orphan spirit, i.e., spiritual immaturity is detailed in Galatians 4:1-3,

"What I am saying is that as long as the heir is a child, he is no different from a slave, although he owns the whole estate. He is subject to guardians and trustees until the time set by his father. So also, when we were children, we were in slavery under the basic principles of the world."

God's original plan was for spiritual fathers to train up the sons of God. These fathers are to "act" on behalf of God the Father. Too many believers cannot receive the love of the Father because they have been personally abused, hurt, rejected and wounded by their earthly fathers or those in spiritual authority over them. They cannot receive the love of their heavenly Father because they cannot bring themselves to a place of being able to trust Him. Trust involves vulnerability. Trust involves giving and receiving. The spiritually immature (those with the orphan spirit) cannot trust or receive until the unhealed issues and hidden cores of pain are attended to.

Basic trust is a real issue in finding a spiritual father who will help you become the son of God you were meant to be. Paul said,

> *"Even though you have ten thousand guardians in Christ, you do not have many fathers, for in Christ Jesus I became your father through the gospel."* (1 Corinthians 4:15)

The word "guardians" is the Greek word: *paidagôgous*. This old Greek word comes from two words, *pais* (boy) and *agôgos* (son). This term was used for the guide or attendant of the child who took him to school as in Galatians 3:24 (schoolmaster) and also as a sort of tutor who had a care for the child when not in school. This would be likened to a school bus driver or day care worker today.

The phrase Paul used in addressing the Corinthians, *"I became your father"* is the Greek phrase: *humas egennêsa*. It meant that Paul was not taking the place of the Heavenly Father or the Lord Jesus, but that He was a spiritual father to them in Christ. The definition of the word "father": (Hebrew *'abba;* Greek *pater*) is from the root word meaning: creator, originator, founder, author, protector, provider, upholder, parent, ruler, and elder. A spiritual father then would be one who has infused his own life into others, such as Abraham being the father of the faithful.

> *"So then, he (Abraham) is the father of all who believe..."* (Romans 4:11)

Such a spiritual connection indicates close resemblance, kinship, and affinity with a spiritual father and causes the father to be seen as:

1. A spiritual source.
2. The inventor originator of a certain pattern of life.
3. One who occupies a position of counsel and care.
4. A revered or honored superior in spiritual things.
5. Complete and mature in their walk with God.
6. Established and confirmed in church doctrine.
7. The author of society of persons animated by the same spirit as himself.
8. One who stands in a father's place and looks after another in a paternal way.

9. Therefore, the duties and character of a true spiritual father would be:

10.   He loves. Genesis 37:4
11.   He commands. Genesis 50:16
12.   He instructs. Proverbs 1:8
13.   He guides, encourages and warns.
       Jeremiah 3:4; 1Thessalonians 2:11
14.   He trains. Hosea 11:3
15.   He rebukes. Genesis 34:30
16.   He restrains. Contrasted in 1 Samuel 3:13
17.   He disciplines. Deuteronomy 8:5
18.   He nourishes. Isaiah 1:2
19.   He delights in his son. Proverbs 3:12
20.   He delights in his son's wisdom. Proverbs 10:1
21.   He is pained by his son's folly. Proverbs 17:25
22.   He is considerate of his son's needs and requests.
       Matthew 7:10
23.   He understands his son's burdens or failures. Malachi 3:17
24.   He is tenderly familiar. Luke 11:7
25.   Considerately self-restrained. Ephesians 6:4

Just as the anointed right thumb of the High Priest touches the remaining fingers, smearing oil upon them, likewise the fathering anointing extends FROM the spiritual father to the his sons enabling them to have the ability to attain the stature of mature children of God. When anything is smeared it becomes unrecognizable. When a spiritual father "smears" a son's life with his anointing the spiritual son will generally become unrecognizable to those who knew him before. **This enables him to be healed and whole. His life and ministry soars to a level never known before. This enables the son to BECOME without fear of failure and thus overcoming the orphan spirit.**

CHAPTER EIGHT

Your Inheritance is in Your True Identity

The development of confidence and passion is essential to embracing and enjoying our promised identity and inheritance. We must first remember that no failure is final. Psalm 73:26 says, *My flesh and my heart may fail, but God is the strength of my heart and my portion forever.* Becoming sons that live out of their true identity doesn't happen without passionate and intentional commitment. One doesn't drift into transformation of soul without choosing, without goals, or without developing a clear plan to follow. Our intention to follow the Lord must involve our whole heart, soul, mind and strength.

Living out of our inheritance must not be viewed with a lukewarm or hapless commitment. Effort must be consistently exerted in the life of a becoming son. Progress involves total devotion, extreme fervor, and passionate zeal. When someone is passionate, they are internally motivated. They give, share their faith, worship, pray, study, engage in world missions— not because they are forced to, or are manipulated into, but because they love the Lord Jesus Christ and their greatest desire is to become a mature son that overcome every obstacle in their way.

What is the reason why so many of God's sons fail in living out of their God given inheritance? Yes, as we discussed before, many feel inadequate and unprepared to be the person God is calling them to be. And many have been hindered by a lack of personal identity. Others have suffered from yeast filled religious philosophy. But the overreaching reason is that many of God's sons are being intimidated by their circumstances or the attitudes of a man centered, need focused and entertainment based Christianity. The "spirit of intimidation" has hindered many a son from "coming out from their past ways" and "coming into their promised inheritance."

The word intimidation means to force one into or deter one from some action by inducing fear or coercion. Sometimes the intimidation comes from the circumstances one has been sent into for the purpose of bringing about maturity. An example of this is found in Matthew 8:25-26,

"The disciples went and woke him, saying, "Lord, save us! We're going to drown!" He replied, "You of little faith, why are you so afraid?" Then he got up and rebuked the winds and the waves, and it was completely calm."

The Lord's disciples could not walk in the inheritance because of the intimidation. Jesus had told them on the western shore of Galilee that they were going to the other side of the lake. After making His declaration, like a mature Son, the Lord went to the stern of the ship to sleep. Weary from the day's activities He slept hard. While sleeping the clouds gathered and a storm common for the Sea of Galilee appeared over the ship as it sailed toward the opposite shore. Within a few minutes the storm became violent. The wind drove the waves over the bow of the ship and it began to sink. Fear filled the hearts of the disciples. Each one began asking who had the courage to wake the Lord and ask for his help. Intimidation had done its work. The taught and trained succumbed to the fear. Finally, they woke the Lord.

The disciples did not understand that the solution to sailing through the storm (circumstances) was given by the Lord before they left the dock. Jesus said, "We are going to the other side." This was a portion of their inheritance. Their lives had been guaranteed until they safely reached the other side of the lake. If the Son of God said they were going to (and reaching) the other side no storm or circumstance could stop them. Whether they stilled the storm, walked on top of the water, divided the water and crossed on dry ground...they were going to the other side of the lake.

Circumstances like these should not affect our lives. We have the promise the disciples had. We are going to become...and nothing shall keep us from our arrival. Through our faith in the Son of God we have been given everlasting life. There will come a time when we will lay down our body but our spirit and soul will live forever. When Christ died on the cross He died not only for us, but as us. Therefore we died when he died. We have been crucified with Him and now the life we live; we live by the life of the Son of God. (Galatians 2:20) The Apostle Peter also said,

"Blessed be the God and Father of our Lord Jesus Christ, which according to his abundant mercy hath begotten us again unto a lively hope by the resurrection of Jesus Christ from the dead, to an inheritance incorruptible, and undefiled, and that fadeth not away, reserved in heaven for you, Who are kept by the power of God through faith unto salvation ready to be revealed in the last time."
(1 Peter 1:3-5)

Our inheritance is not earthy. It cannot rust or be stolen. Our inheritance is our promised victory. *For whatsoever is born of God overcometh the world: and this is the victory that overcometh the world, even our faith.* (1 John 5:4) The word "overcometh" is from the Greek word *nikao* (nik-ah'-o) which means: to conquer, to carry off the victory, or to come off victorious. For believers, victory is sure. Sons of God hold fast to their faith even unto death whether the battle is against the power of their foes, temptations or persecutions.

God is not a man that He should lie. His promises are yes and amen. He will never leave us or forsake us. Hallelujah!

The attack of intimidation upon a son's identity and inheritance can also come by way of ungodly people. During the time of the Judges the Midianites came up with their livestock and their tents like swarms of locusts. The scripture says that it was impossible to count the men and their camels; they invaded the land of Israel to ravage it. The Midianites so impoverished the Israelites that God's people cried out to the LORD for help. This intimidation by the Midianites put God's people in a place where they believed the land given to them by the Lord was about to be lost forever.

God's answer was Gideon. God chose someone who was the most intimidated to overthrow the intimidators. When addressed by the angel of the Lord Gideon declared he was from the smallest tribe. He also was from the smallest family and the youngest son. He was hiding from the enemy. He was afraid. He was afraid because he could not see his real identity nor embrace his everlasting inheritance.

The angel of the Lord came and called him "a mighty man of courage." God called Gideon a mighty man (true identity) though he exhibited the traits of a coward. The intimidating power of the Midianites had stolen Gideon's freedom, prosperity and victory (inheritance).

Finally when Gideon decided to answer God's call God again showed Gideon the power of his identity as well as the size of his inheritance. God sent home all who were infected with the disease (cowardice) that haunted Gideon. Simply put, they were afraid. (22,000 men) He also sent home all of those who didn't drink by lapping the water from their hand (10,000 more). Gideon was allowed to only keep 300 men. These 300 men didn't win the battle. The battle was won by the power of the promise given to Abraham, lived through Isaac, Israel, and Joshua. With the promise came the land. The land (the place of their becoming and the life to be lived on it) was the inheritance and it belonged to God's people.

According to Judges 7:19-21;

> *"Gideon, and the hundred men that were with him, came unto the outside of the camp in the beginning of the middle watch; and they had but newly set the watch: and they blew the trumpets, and broke the pitchers that were in their hands. And the three companies blew the trumpets, and broke the pitchers, and held the lamps in their left hands, and the trumpets in their right hands to blow withal: and they cried the sword of the LORD, and of Gideon. And they stood every man in his place round about the camp: and the entire host ran, and cried, and fled."*

Do you see your inheritance in this story? As I stated in the introduction God is more interested in who we become than what we become. The things that happen within us are much more important than the things that happen to us. God's sons have a promise and a picture within them. It is the becoming of that promised picture that is your inheritance.

Along with the stories of the disciples on the Sea of Galilee and Gideon there are many other ways God's people are intimidated into giving up their inheritance. Peter suffered intimidation from the threat of personal exposure.

> *"You also were with Jesus of Galilee," she said. But he denied it before them all. "I don't know what you're talking about," he said. Then he went out to the gateway, where another girl saw him and said to the people there, "This fellow was with Jesus of Nazareth." He denied it again, with an oath: "I don't know the man!" Then Peter remembered the word Jesus had spoken: "Before the rooster crows, you will disown me three times." And he went outside and wept bitterly."* (Matthew 26:69-75)

Daniel was threatened with physical harm by Nebuchadnezzar.

> *"But if you do not worship it, you will be thrown immediately into a blazing furnace. Then what god will be able to rescue you from my hand?"* (Daniel 3:14-15)

So were Shadrach, Meshach and Abednego.

> *"Nebuchadnezzar spake and said unto them, 'Is it true, O Shadrach, Meshach, and Abednego, do not ye serve my gods, nor*

worship the golden image which I have set up? Now if ye be ready that at what time ye hear the sound of the cornet, flute, harp, sackbut, psaltery, and dulcimer, and all kinds of music, ye fall down and worship the image which I have made; well: but if ye worship not, ye shall be cast the same hour into the midst of a burning fiery furnace; and who is that God that shall deliver you out of my hands?'" (Daniel 3:14-15)

Sons have also been intimidated by the direct spiritual attack of the adversary, the devil.

"The thief comes only to steal and kill and destroy;"
(John 10:10)
"Be sober, be vigilant; because your adversary the devil, as a roaring lion, walketh about, seeking whom he may devour."
(1 Peter 5:8)

Perhaps still more have been affected by the talent, giftedness or success of others. The spies sent by Moses into the Promised Land were also intimidated into giving up on their inheritance. As I discussed previously, ten of the men felt that though God had brought them out of Egypt, through the Red Sea, across the wilderness, providing manna for bread, quail for meat and water from the Rock; God either could not or would not enable them to overcome the enemy. They disbelieved the promise spoken into the ears of their ancestors and sons. These men became weak in their faith. Their faith deformed into chaos. They chose to surrender the very thing promised to them. And they spread among the Israelites a bad report about the land they had explored. They said,

"The land we explored devours those living in it. All the people we saw there are of great size." (Numbers 13:32)

Finally, there are many sons who are intimidated by the perceived or real lack of acceptance by others. When God spoke to Moses about returning to Egypt and freeing the Israelites from their bondage Moses responded with,

"What if they do not believe me or listen to me and say, 'The LORD did not appear to you'?" (Exodus 4:1)

I want to share with you the truth concerning the coming out of and overcoming the intimidation that would destroy your identity and inheritance. First, son of God, come to the understanding that,

"God has not given us the spirit of intimidation, but a spirit of power, of love, and of self-discipline." (2 Timothy 1:7)

Through self-discipline we "grow up" (become) to a level of maturity that enables us to live our lives not as servants, but as sons. (Galatians 4:1-3)

Possessing God's confidence is the answer to being intimidated. David said,

The LORD is my light and my salvation-- whom shall I fear?
The LORD is the stronghold of my life-- of whom shall I be afraid?

David displayed tremendous confidence in the Lord and in himself. David found the secret of confidence being the foundational attitude for walking in his inheritance. Confidence is much more than having a positive attitude. It is more than having faith in God. Confidence is knowing The Son and knowing that you are a son!

David wrote in Psalm 27:1-3,

"The LORD is my light and my salvation-- whom shall I fear?
The LORD is the stronghold of my life-- of whom shall I be afraid?
When evil men advance against me to devour my flesh, when my
enemies and my foes attack me, they will stumble and fall. Though
an army besiege me, my heart will not fear; though war break out
against me, even then will I be confident."

David spent time being in the presence of the Lord through prayer and praise. Such intimate moments caused David to come to the saving, healing and delivering knowledge of the Lord. He came to the understanding that a relationship with the Lord brought great rewards. The rewards included the Lord's closeness as well as protection, guidance, strength and power.

David also knew that the Hebrew word translated "confidence" meant "to be open," showing consequently the thought that originated the idea of "confidence" in the Hebrew mind; where there was nothing hidden a person felt safe; because of this confidence is very frequently rendered "trust" in the scriptures.

This was the same theme of the Apostle Paul who wrote,

"For I am convinced that neither death nor life, neither angels
nor demons, neither the present nor the future, nor any powers,
neither height nor depth, nor anything else in all creation, will be
able to separate us from the love of God that is in Christ Jesus our
Lord." (Romans 8:38-39)

A son's confidence develops when they have complete trust in the Lord and in themselves. This trust is rewarded with being abundantly satisfied and blessed.

Confidence flows out of the development of our true identity and the building of spiritual intimacy with the Lord. Prophets Isaiah and Jeremiah spoke prophetic words that speak to the confidence of God's sons. Godly confidence is the result of the righteousness found in our relationship with God. The deeper our relationship, the deeper the righteousness and righteousness affects the way we see ourselves, as well as our circumstances and problems. When we see ourselves as becoming God's son, holy peace is produced within. Isaiah prophesied,

"The fruit of righteousness will be peace; the effect of righteousness will be quietness and confidence forever."
(Isaiah 32:17)

The scripture assures us that confidence creates the blessing of the Lord. The blessing of the Lord causes us to be like trees planted by the water. Roots grow deep into the stream. When opposition comes, there is no fear. Even in a year of drought, the confident son never fails to bear fruit. (Jeremiah 17:7-8)

As heirs and joint heirs with Christ we are partakers of the divine nature of God. His nature is at work in us. His nature has empowered us refute death, defeat, and confusion. His nature empowers us to embrace the essence of our inheritance, which is life, joy and peace. This reality is not some futuristic hope, it is a now message, a word of life for today. It is a working and transforming message for every son of God.

We are different for having heard it, better for having believed it, and changed more into His image for having received it. Our inheritance grows as the Son's life is established in every area of our lives. I know that greater things are ahead of us than the human race has ever seen before. There is a bright tomorrow for those who enter their inheritance. The sons of God shall know and understand more of the mysteries of God. But these mysteries will be revealed to and understood by those who are faithful to receive that which is being revealed now for today. Take courage, sons of God, for our God is on the Throne! He rules all forces. Nothing can stay His hand. Bless His wonderful Name!

CHAPTER NINE

Impartation and Intimacy

"For you did not receive a spirit that makes you a slave again to fear, but you received the Spirit of sonship. And by him we cry, "Abba, Father." (Romans 8:15)

Sonship is the nature and condition of the true disciples in Christ, who by receiving the Spirit of God into their souls become sons of God. With sonship involves the power of spiritual impartation.

Paul told the Romans,

"For I long to see you, that I may impart unto you some spiritual gift, to the end ye may be established; That is, that I may be comforted together with you by the mutual faith both of you and me." (Romans 1:11-12)

The purpose of this impartation was to establish them. The Greek word for establish is *sterizo*. It means to make stable, place firmly, set fast, fix, strengthen, make firm and constant.

In contrast, the Corinthians sought impartation for the purpose of demonstrating whatever spiritual gift they desired to be in their lives. The Corinthian church was full of members who, just as they elevated their favorite preacher above any other preacher, also elevated their personal gifting as the source of their identity. Evidently many of the Corinthian Christians prophesied or spoke in tongues and felt that their gift was not only greater than the others, but that they themselves were more important than others because of their gifting. The resulting use of charismatic gifts as a mark of identity, instead of as a ministry to the body, caused the confusion and indecency present within their congregational gatherings.

Sadly, today most believers seek impartation from one of their "spiritual heroes" and find their identity in either their gifting (i.e. the Corinthians, chapter 12) or their theological or denominational affiliation (i.e. the Corinthians, chapter one). Out of such disorder most create their own identities. They call themselves everything from apostle to prophetess; pastor to son and everything in between. Realizing one's true spiritual identity can only come as we submit to the impartation of Kingdom Order found in a spiritual father.

We see such an impartation in the life of the Pattern Son, the Lord Jesus Christ. Three times the Heavenly Father spoke over Him and by His words imparted strength for the Lord's ministry and passion. The Father spoke over His Son at His Baptism, on the Mount of Transfiguration and in the Temple at Jerusalem. Each time was a critical moment in the life of the Son. The first time the Son was beginning His earthly ministry. The second came when the Son met with Moses and Elijah to discuss His death and resurrection. The final time came days before Jesus spoke His final words to His disciples, was crucified and then rose from the dead.

It is important for a spiritual father to "speak over" his son imparting and infusing to him the strength, confidence and stability to continue becoming. Such impartation answers the following questions for the son's life.

1. Who am I? *This has to do with our identity.*
2. Where am I from? *This has to do with our heritage.*
3. Why am I here? *This has to do with our purpose in life.*
4. What can I really do? *This has to do with reaching our full potential.*
5. Where am I supposed to go? *This has to do with our destiny in life.*

Through a father's impartation a son is able to give and share himself. This comes at a cost as like the impartation of life that every branch places in the fruit that it bears. Naturally speaking, every father imparts his DNA into his son. Whether that father is natural or spiritual when he establishes and maintains a healthy relationship with his son he also imparts his life, his love and his experience.

Spiritually speaking a spiritual father imparts his "spirit."

"And it came to pass, when they were gone over, that Elijah said unto Elisha, Ask what I shall do for thee, before I be taken away from thee. And Elisha said, I pray thee, let a double portion of thy spirit be upon me." (2 Kings 2:9)

A spiritual father also imparts his life or giftedness.

"For this reason I remind you to fan into flame the gift of God, which is in you through the laying on of my hands. (2 Timothy 1:6)

I long to see you so that I may impart to you some spiritual gift to make you strong." (Romans 1:11)

A spiritual father should also impart his love or grace.

We were not looking for praise from men, not from you or anyone else. As apostles of Christ we could have been a burden to you, but we were gentle among you, like a mother caring for her little children. (1 Thessalonians 2:6-7)

A spiritual father must impart his experience or ways.

"For this reason I am sending to you Timothy, my son whom I love, who is faithful in the Lord. He will remind you of my way of life in Christ Jesus, which agrees with what I teach everywhere in every church." (1 Corinthians 4:17)

Today there are thousands of people in ministry who have been educated in the finest schools. Many have supplemented their formal education through audiotapes, videotapes and the internet as well as from books and magazines from qualified scholarly sources. Although there has never been a greater flood of biblical material available, there are precious few drops of biblical power manifested. We reach millions with information, but without spiritual relationship, impartational truth cannot be given nor received. The reason we have not seen a manifestation of power in biblical proportions is because we are not giving and receiving impartation by biblical pattern. We have ten thousand boy-sons in Christ but not many fathers.

Spiritual impartation is also the process whereby the Lord produces security in the life of the becoming son. This security is found in his beliefs, behaviors, opinions, and character. A becoming son must receive the much needed strength to follow the patterns in the scriptures (the way one sees things), to submit to scriptural alignment (the way one thinks), to embrace their spiritual uniqueness (who they are in Christ), and to learn to trust their Heavenly Father concerning what He desires them to become.

Sonship involves being open to the influence only a spiritual father can bring. This kind of trust involves opening one's heart to a spiritual father. Spiritual orphans have closed their hearts because they are afraid of being hurt. They refuse to make themselves vulnerable because of past hurts and pain. Their spirits are closed to a love relationship with their heavenly Father because they do not trust Him. Instead of running to God, they are continually running away from Him. Because of their trust issues a son must be willing to accept the influence of a father beyond the surface.

Spiritual orphans are dysfunctional because they lack the basic trust needed to have healthy relationships with those in authority. They find themselves battling with fear, control issues, independence and pride. They are not able to have intimate relationships because they are not able to receive comfort or love from God or others.

Insecure sons focus on:	Confident sons focus on:
Being ordinary	Becoming extraordinary
Their Limitations	God's Expectations
Meeting man's standards	Setting Standards for others
Getting through	Breaking through
Learning as effort	Learning as enjoyable
Blaming the past	Planning the future
Pointing the finger	Being accountable

We have used the term "spiritual orphan" in this material to describe how many of sons relate to God the Father on the basis of works or earning God's love, acceptance and approval. Although as sons we have been adopted into the family of God, we still behave like "orphans" and like we have no intimacy with Christ.

Spiritual intimacy moves a becoming son past the outer courts and into the Most Holy Place of God's Presence. It involves getting beyond the "door" mentality and entering into a more mature view of salvation and sanctification. It also involves revelation, illumination and worship as a lifestyle instead of an event, which causes the becoming son to live in the presence of God.

Intimacy also means submitting to a father's authority. Such submission is a result of the closeness and honesty that develops when both the father and the son are willing to be humble, vulnerable and no longer hide or deny their emotional pain. Such intimacy replaces the comfort and identity found in...

➢ Money (the possession of things)
➢ Addictions (alcohol, drugs, food, immorality)
➢ Position (striving to be seen, noticed and accepted)
➢ Power (by controlling their own lives)

Intimacy also replaces religious activity with relationship. Love is no longer earned, but received. Religion is replaced by love, acceptance and forgiveness. Intimacy overcomes the "orphan spirit. Intimacy overcomes the inability to have lasting relationships, the hatred of authority, general distrust for sons, the general lack of direction and the inability to make key, strategic decisions.

CHAPTER TEN

Becoming a Righteous Seed

"A spiritual father is someone whose life and ministry raised you up from the mire of immaturity into exciting spiritual growth and Kingdom order." Kathie Eads

Samuel was the son of Hannah, but in understanding his responsibility he replaced sons who were older than himself, this was because Eli's natural sons did not accept their TRUE SPIRITUAL IDENTITY. Therefore Samuel's responsibility became that of replacing unrighteous seed with righteous seed.

The same is true of the Lord Jesus. Adam lost his TRUE SPIRITUAL IDENTITY as God's seed, but the Lord Jesus Christ (the Pattern Son) came, who is the last Adam, to replace the unrighteous seed with righteous seed.

We reproduce who we are. Every son's responsibility is to become a righteous seed. If a son doesn't become a righteous seed, what will they reproduce? Unrighteousness! On the other hand, sons of Adam can only reproduce unrighteous seed, but the sons of God as a righteous seed can only reproduce righteous seed. Those who are in Christ are righteous, not because of themselves, but because of the seed they were born from. We can only produce righteousness if we are a righteous seed.

A righteous seed is able to "carry on" the life of his spiritual father. Both Joshua and Elisha continued what Moses and Elijah had started. In fact, they built upon what they had been given and where their predecessors had brought God's people out of bondage and apostasy, they were able to bring them into freedom and righteousness. In both instances the father brought God's people out of something and the son finished the course by bringing them into something better.

And he brought us out from thence, that he might bring us in, to give us the land which he sware unto our fathers. Deuteronomy 6:23

Elisha asked for the eldest son's inheritance. He asked to "carry on" the life and ministry of Elijah and did so when he cried, "My father, my father." Elisha also tore his clothes (identity) off. He did not keep his clothes under his father's mantle thus keeping his own agenda. He did not wear his clothes over his father's mantle thus acting as though he had nothing to complete. He did not pick up the mantle of his father until he had gotten rid of his own. His mantle was not large enough to handle his father's anointing.

"When they had crossed, Elijah said to Elisha, "Tell me, what can I do for you before I am taken from you?" "Let me inherit a double portion of your spirit," Elisha replied. "You have asked a difficult thing," Elijah said, "yet if you see me when I am taken from you, it will be yours-- otherwise not." As they were walking along and talking together, suddenly a chariot of fire and horses of fire appeared and separated the two of them, and Elijah went up to heaven in a whirlwind. Elisha saw this and cried out, "My father! My father! The chariots and horsemen of Israel!" And Elisha saw him no more. Then he took hold of his own clothes and tore them apart." (2 Kings 2:9-12)

Another example of a son finishing the vision of his father is Solomon. God did not give Solomon his own vision; God gave the vision to David his father. Solomon's responsibility was to finish the vision that God had given to David. Whatever vision is left undone by your spiritual father, it is a son's responsibility to finish that vision.

Just as Solomon's responsibility was to build the Temple, but it was his father, David, who had the responsibility to see that Solomon had all the materials to build the vision. David built up the store, he assembled everything that was needed to build the Temple, but He didn't build it. His son, Solomon built it. In the same way, as a spiritual son, your responsibility is to finish your father's vision.

Becoming a righteous seed establishes unity between a father and son. Unity is a sign of spiritual maturity, where disunity is a sign of carnality. (1 Corinthians 3:1-3) Unity also strengthens the Church and brings about the "one mind" that produces miracles and great power. God wants spiritual sons that are of one spiritual mind and purpose with a spiritual father – while exercising their varying gifts and ministries.

How does a son build a spiritual agreement with a spiritual father? Spiritual agreement begins in the "heart and soul" (Acts 4:32) and involves being of "one mind" so that we are one, just as the Father and the Son are one. This is a lot more than agreeing on doctrine! It even extended to sharing possessions!

1. Share your testimonies so you can truly know each other.

2. Pray about each other's life concerns.

3. Meet regularly and for at least an hour each time.

4. Keep a prayer journal – requests, date, date answered.

5. Worship together.

6. Eat together. Sharing vision, dreams and plans.

7. Hear from God together. Spend some time listening to God.

8. Explore biblical truth together.

9. Appreciate one another's gifts.

10. Be vulnerable to one another's strengths.

11. Exercise patience and forbearance.

12. Raise questions about "new teachings" or strange and controversial   matters.

13. Study the Scriptures as to your relationship.

14. Put away pride, envy and selfish ambition.

15. Keep a lid on your anger and speak the truth in love.

16. Apologize quickly. Keep short accounts with God and with each other.

17. Keep in touch by phone, email etc.

18. Ask the tough questions about common purpose and pace.

19. Decide that you will always work things out.

20. Beware of being disappointed with one another.

21. Do not complain.

22. Develop a spiritual sensitivity to the presence of unity and spiritual agreement and maintain it.

CHAPTER ELEVEN

Transformational Thinking

The Bible refers to the cultivation and development of a son of God's true becoming as being "*transformed by the renewing of your mind.*" (Romans 12:1-2) Most sons allow their minds to be filled with thoughts of doubt, fear, inability, insecurity, worry, and defeat. In our becoming sons of God this negativism must be flushed out, and the mind saturated with the positive Word and Spirit of the Lord.

A person literally is what he thinks and believes. His life is the sum total of his thoughts. Each of us are today what our thoughts, beliefs, and convictions have made us. What we think and say about our circumstances and problems is of vital importance in overcoming them, and often learning to re-think our identity spells the difference between victory and defeat.

Thoughts and feelings of inadequacy can keep a son of God from reaching their full potential. Sadly, many people war against a persistent and deep rooted sense of personal inadequacy resulting in the tendency to diminish oneself, this develops shyness and timidity, or excessively aggressive behavior through overcompensation. There are several underlying reasons for this. The first is consistent disapproval from parents, peers, teachers and church sons. Perhaps this includes you. Have you been one who has received negative input throughout your childhood? Were you told that you were an unwanted baby or that you were never as good as a sibling? Maybe you remember seldom being praised for your accomplishments or never feeling like you were able to please your parents. An example is that if you came home with a report card and on it were all A's and one B, and instead of praise for the A's, the question was asked, "Why didn't you get an A in this subject too?"

I have ministered to hundreds of pastors and ministers who either experienced unbalanced parental approval or they had an abnormal amount of control exercised over them. If a child is told how wonderful and superior they are, but they are never taught how to deal with their weaknesses in a constructive manner, feelings of inferiority can surface. These feelings cry out for an abnormal amount of approval. Also, there appears to be many who had a mother or father who were overly critical and controlling of their children. But this is not found in parent-child relationships. It also can happen if a spouse or spiritual son keeps giving you the message that you can't do anything right. Somewhere along the way, a teacher or a coach may have been overbearing or controlling resulting in a negative self-image.

What is the result of being controlled, manipulated, or having to deal with the idea that we are not good enough? First of all these types of experiences usually result in the desire to conform to what appears to be the norm. This gives way to a tendency to be always comparing ourselves with others and causes a person to emphasize the negative aspects of one's life and personality. Hiding and being shy is another form of dealing with this problem as well as speaking continuous negative self-talk to one's self. The Bible teaches that, *"As a man thinks in his heart, so is he."* Thoughts like these usually manifest themselves through procrastination, depression and the avoidance of confrontation.

Now you may have been vulnerable to inferior feelings at some time or other, but you don't have to let them take up permanent residence in your life. God has made each of us unique, different from everyone else, with both superior and inferior skills. Our capabilities, however, have nothing to do with the intrinsic value God has placed on us.

When Jesus was here on earth, He welcomed all sorts of people— fishermen, tax collectors, prostitutes, housewives, rulers, and the rich and the poor. He died for each one of us. God's price tag on us will never change, no matter how skillful or unskillful we are. Each of us is a one-of-a-kind person, and we will never be less valuable or more valuable to God than we are right now. The Prophet Jeremiah appears to have faced the difficulty of overcoming inferiority. All through his book, you will find that Jeremiah is very honest about his feelings. He began his ministry as a timid, gentle, sensitive, emotional young man on whom God had laid His hand for a specific purpose.

Jeremiah was overwhelmed with his assignment. His response? *"Lord, I do not know how to speak; I am only a child."* God immediately answered Him:

"Do not say 'I am only a child! You must go to everyone I send you to and say whatever I command you. Do not be afraid of them, for I am with you and will rescue you." (Jeremiah 1:7)

What happened next must have been truly astonishing. Jeremiah said,

"Then the LORD reached out his hand and touched my mouth and said to me, 'Now, I have put my words in your mouth. See, today I appoint you over nations and kingdoms to uproot and tear down, to destroy and overthrow, to build and to plant.'"
(Jeremiah 1:7-10)

The Lord made a declaration that transformed Jeremiah's becoming. The character of this declaration was by no means merely a prediction. It was more than "hope so." That which was given by the Lord to the young prophet referred to his becoming and how it was to relate to his present as well as to his future. However, that which was revealed to Jeremiah finds its inner unity in this…that it was all aimed to establish the preeminence of the Lord God and to establish the Kingdom of God in a greater dimension within the hearts of men through the life and ministry of Jeremiah.

God was speaking of future events in their relation to God's divine plan, and the ultimate purpose of this was the absolute establishment of the supremacy of Jehovah's Kingdom in the earth. Some of the transformation principles that changed Jeremiah were that:

> Transformational thinking is "history in reverse." God wanted Jeremiah to learn to see and speak of the future in present tense.
> Jeremiah was to view himself as God saw him. He had been appointed and given a destiny that would transform God's children for thousands of years.
> There are no limitations to those who are the Lord's and are called according to His purpose.
> Becoming a son of God involves more than human reason. Transformation of our thinking enables the human mind to transcend its own finite limitations and come away with the belief that all things are possible.

Transformation of thought is not the acknowledgement or acceptance of simple information, but it is the presentation and invasion of The Lord and His Kingdom into our lives. It is the impartation of the life, death and resurrection of our Lord that first gives new understanding to the understanding needed to transform our thinking. In the person who is in Christ Jesus, this transformation is not merely an experience, but the act of the Lord being experienced, of being exposed to, of being called upon, where we are overwhelmed and taken over by Him who seeks to reveal Himself.

Through such thinking the indescribable becomes a voice, disclosing that God is not a being that is apart from His people. He is not an enigma, but justice, mercy, and love. He is not only the power to which we are accountable, but also the pattern for our lives. He is not the "unknown"; He is the Father, the God of Abraham; out of the endless ages He comes with compassion and guidance. It is through this way of thought that we are able to encounter The Lord as the "Being" beyond the mystery we call "life".

God also told Jeremiah three important things here that would sustain him for the rest of his life. These same principles can help us find the confidence we need to overcome our own sense of inadequacy or feelings of inferiority and see these feelings replaced by transformational thinking.

First, Jeremiah was under God's authority. Jeremiah did not have to work on sermons or solicit speaking invitations. God would send him where he wanted him to go, and God would tell him the words to say. God had chosen Jeremiah to be His prophet, so he was acting under God's authority and with His power.

Second, Jeremiah was protected by God's Presence. God told Jeremiah, "Do not be afraid of them." The reason Jeremiah didn't have to fear anyone was because God had promised His constant presence and protection, assuring him, "I will be with you and will rescue you."

Finally, God was the source of Jeremiah's ability. In his vision, Jeremiah saw God reach out and touch his mouth to symbolically demonstrate that he was now God's spokesman. His feelings of inadequacy and inferiority were justified in his own strength, but the Lord made it clear to him that He would give him the ability and the power to do the job he was being commissioned to do.

Jeremiah overcame by believing God's words. He depended on God to protect him. He had God's guarantee, His promises. God kept His promises and made Jeremiah a powerful prophet for the rest of his life.

As Paul said,

"Such confidence as this is ours through Christ before God. Not that we are competent in ourselves to claim anything for ourselves, but our competence comes from God" (2 Corinthians 3:4,5)

Jesus said,

"Apart from me you can do nothing!" (John 15:5)

The Precious and Powerful Holy Spirit lives within us. The same Person who empowered the Lord Jesus in His ministry is in residence in our hearts and minds. By embracing the becoming God has for us the Holy Spirit opens God's Word to us. He motivates us to obey it. He puts His thoughts into our minds. He desires to give us the words to say and enables those words with supernatural power. He invests Himself in our every act of service and obedience with eternal value and impact.

Such transformation brings the realization that God is the One who makes us want to do His will, and He gives us the ability to perform it. We can depend on our loving Savior for strength; He never gets tired or impatient with us. When God gives us a task, He gives us the ability to do it. He provides the encouragement and the help we need to persevere.

I hope that you are reaching out to the Holy Spirit and asking Him to help you develop the self-confidence to crystallize your thinking and establish an exact direction for your own life. Commit yourself to moving in the direction He desires for you, and then take the determined action to acquire, accomplish and become the will of God. Choose to become by building on your current strengths rather than attempting to improve apparent weaknesses.

Focus on being "a meaningful specific" rather than "a wandering generality." Decide to confront yourself concerning your own untapped potential. It has been said that we use only about 15% of our potential. There is great sadness found in graveyards because about the 85% of man's potential is buried there!

It is important that we understand how transformational thinking is fully developed. The goals we achieve in life are a mirror of what we see in ourselves. In the illustration below, we see how our thinking ultimately determines who we are and what we do.

Results: Sum of Who We Are and What We Do
⇧
Habits: Compression of Actions
⇧
Actions: Expression of Words and Opinions
⇧
Words: Expression of Attitudes and Beliefs
⇧
Thoughts: Beliefs You Would Change with More
                Information
⇧
Conditioning: How you see yourself through
                Impartation and Intimacy

So, how do we fully develop thinking that is correct for a son of God?

First, we must be "re-conditioned." Throughout this book I have shared that much of what we think today has to do with what we were told and taught to think yesterday. As small children we valued the acceptance of our parents, teachers, pastors and friends. Sadly, most of humanity has been conditioned to expect the negative in almost every area of life.

When we were first learning to pull ourselves up to a table covered with curious and mystical things we automatically reached out to touch, feel and discover. For most of us someone (probably a parent) said, "No, no! Don't touch." This was followed by teachers who told us not to color outside the lines, pastors who spoke more about what would send us to hell than teaching us how to bring heaven to earth. Peers made fun when we were too slow, too fat, or too thin.

What are we to do? We must accept the finished work of the Lord Jesus Christ. What is that work? That all sin past, present and future has been eternally dealt with. God has redeemed us from the power, presence and penalty of sin. We are not to try to "better" our old nature. We are to count ourselves dead to sin and dead to our past. We have been resurrected unto everlasting life. We are new creatures. The old man has passed away and all things have become new.

We must sow good seed-thoughts. The Apostle Paul speaks to this in Philippians 4:8;

> *"Finally, brothers, whatever is true, whatever is noble, whatever is right, whatever is pure, whatever is lovely, whatever is admirable- if anything is excellent or praiseworthy—think about such things."*

A son of God must form the habit of saturating their mind with the positive promises of God at the start of each day. We must refuse the negative thoughts of fear, worry, anxiety, doubt, and defeat from entering our mind. The first thoughts that impress themselves upon our consciousness as we wake up each day are of vital importance, because these "seeds" of thought will affect your Self Image the entire day. I use the following seed thoughts at the start of my day...

> *"I am a new creation."* (2 Corinthians 5:17)
>
> *"I am fearfully and wonderfully made."* (Psalm 139:14)
>
> *"The joy of the Lord is my strength."* (Nehemiah 8:10)
>
> *"The Lord is my helper, and I will not fear."* (Hebrews 13:6)
>
> *"This is the day the Lord has made; I will rejoice and be glad."* (Psalm 118:24)
>
> *"God will be with me and deliver me. (Psalm 91:15)"*
>
> *"I can run through a troop and leap over a wall."* (Psalm 18:29)

"I am more than a conqueror through Christ." (Romans 8:37)
"I can do everything through him who strengthens me."
(Philippians 4:13)

Remember, too, He has promised,

"Fear thou not; for I am with thee: be not dismayed; for I am thy God: I will strengthen thee; yea, I will help thee; yea, I will uphold thee with the right hand of my righteousness.... When thou pass through the waters, I will be with thee; and through the rivers, they shall not overflow thee: when thou walk through the fire, thou shall not be burned; neither shall the flame kindle upon thee" (Isaiah 41:10 and 43:2)

The next step is to cultivate the garden of your mind. Our minds are like gardens. They must be cultivated or else the weeds of inferiority will take root and grow. We therefore deliberately choose positive thoughts and sow the right seed. Then we must weed out all the "weed seeds" that others would plant. This means that there are times we must refuse the words of others and remove all the critical, impure, doubtful, and fearful words that others have spoken into our lives followed by focusing on the goodness and greatness of God. Paul tells us in Ephesians 5:26 to, "wash out your mind with the water of the Word." And Jude tells us to water the good seed by praying in and with the Spirit. (Jude 20)

It is said that people do not plan to fail but a lot of people fail to plan. To become a mature son we must take the time each day to take control of the most precious resource at our command, the next twenty-four hours. Without a plan for the day, one can easily get distracted, spending time serving the loudest voice rather than attending to the most important things for the day that will enhance our identity.

Without written goals our thinking is likened to the electricity in a summer thunderstorm, powerful and exciting, but lacking purpose and direction. Goals serve as a filter to eliminate irrelevant demands. Goals bring to life order, meaning, and purpose that sustain interest and increases motivation over time. Goals express the desire to achieve, to improve, as well as to be changed into the image of God's Dear Son.

When you know who you are, recognize your strengths, and understand what is important in life, you are in a position to organize your thinking. Such thinking reduces conflict and identifies priorities.

Like the Prophet Jeremiah transformational thinking stimulates visualization. When we have clear thoughts and actions for achieving our God identity our commitment becomes firm. This commitment makes goals clear and vivid, which act as a magnetic force to pull us forward. Our thoughts and words become a self-fulfilling prophecy. We gain from life exactly what we plan and expect.

CHAPTER TWELVE

The Corporate Son

"Remember the former things, those of long ago; I am God, and there is no other; I am God, and there is none like me. I make known the end from the beginning, from ancient times, what is still to come. I say: My purpose will stand, and I will do all that I please. From the east I summon a bird of prey; from a far-off land, a man to fulfill my purpose. What I have said, that will I bring about; what I have planned, that will I do." (Isaiah 46:9-11)

The fulfillment of God's purpose is known as the ministry of the Spirit. The purpose of this ministry is to break the power of darkness, invoke the power of light and to bring sons into complete union with the Son. This union is nothing more than the perfecting of our identity in Christ Jesus. This purpose may not be readily recognized. While we may feel that our true loyalty is to Christ, in the lives of most believers, it is the traditions we have grown up with that have become more important than the purposes of Christ Himself.

The second purpose is to join us to the Lord's Body. Generally what we have been taught in Christianity is to see in our mind's eye just "Jesus and me." In our becoming, His purpose is for us to be joined to other believers. All believers are called to be-coming the Body of Christ. Then as we all, begin beholding the face of the Lord and being transformed into the image of God's dear Son, we discover to our joy and amazement that His purpose is for us to be in union and fellowship with others.

It is then we find out that others are being likewise taught and disciplined in their individual relationship with Him. It is here that a revelation occurs. We see ourselves as a stream or channel only to be joined to other streams or waters (believers) for the purpose of eventually flowing together with all believers as the great river of God, which is full of water (spirit) and will bless all humanity.

There are many scriptures that give us a picture of our new corporate identity. Starting with:

Psalm 46:4 *"There is a river, the streams whereof shall make glad the city of God, the holy place of the tabernacles of The Most High."*

I want you to notice that the use of the word "river" is singular. Throughout the bible the Holy Spirit is typified as the river of God. He is especially pictured in the vision in Ezekiel chapter 47. The river of God flows out from the heavenly temple growing as it goes. When measured, the river is first to the ankles, then to the knees and loins and finally water to swim in. This prophetic picture tells us that anything the river touches is brought to life which is representative of our eternal salvation found in Christ Jesus.

When we examine this verse in Psalms more closely we see that the word translated "streams" is plural. This speaks of the tributaries of the Holy Spirit that flow out of our inner most beings. (John 7:37-39)The bible teaches Jesus Christ is the Pattern Son and we who believe on Him, the Corporate Son who is "altogether lovely. " (SOS 5:16)We are many members in one body, and all members have not the same office: So we, *being* many, are one body in Christ, and every one members one of another. (Romans 12:4-5)

Our corporate identity is then described in the scriptures as being "waters."

Genesis 1:2 *"And the earth was without form, and void; and darkness was upon the face of the deep. And the Spirit of God moved upon the face of the waters."*

Isaiah 8:6 *"Forasmuch as this people refuseth the waters of Shiloah that go softly."*

Isaiah 55:1 *"Ho, every one that thirsteth, come ye to the waters, and he that hath no money; come ye, buy, and eat; yea, come, buy wine and milk without money and without price."*

Psalm 105:41 *"He opened the rock, and the waters gushed out; they ran in the dry places like a river."*

We, the waters, streams, and tributaries flow out from within and come together. Together, this river flows into the ocean and from the ocean comes the clouds that bring rain upon the land. The purpose of the rain is not merely to replenish the rivers that flow back into the oceans. But God desires to accomplish His will through a many membered body. Beyond our individual purpose He desires that in our coming together He can "water the earth" that it may bring forth and bud. And after the budding, He wants the fruit. That He may give seed to the sower and bread to the eater. The ultimate purpose is that we live for others. We learn to pour our lives out so that others may be healed and blessed.

Another picture of corporate identity is found in Psalm 40:7-8;

*"Then said I, Lo, I come: in the **volume** of the book it is written of me, I delight to do thy will, O my God: yea, thy law is within my heart."*

The beginning of John's Gospel declares that Jesus Christ is The Word. Individually, we are His letters or words. (2 Corinthians 3:2)Each of us are one of the eight parts of speech. Alone, we tell little of the goodness of our Lord. Arranged in correct sequence we become phrases, sentences, paragraphs and chapters of "His-story. "Some of us are nouns, others verbs, adjectives or conjunctions. Together, we make up the declaration of God's expression in the earth. The earth is waiting with expectation for such a manifestation of the sons of God.

I have learned that almost all people will never embrace corporate identity without realizing their individual identity as a son of God. Without the power to overcome inferiority, false identity and the belief that each of us are incapable of great things, we will be fearful of coming together. This fear conveys itself through timidity or false arrogance making many fearful of being "lost in the crowd. "

The Apostle Paul exhorts us in Romans and the first letter to the Corinthians to come to the understanding that all the members of the body are needed. The hand cannot say to the foot, "I have no need of you. "The more visible parts cannot do away with that part which cannot be seen. Each of us are unique. Each of us are special. God did not make us to be clones of one "super saint. "He created us to be exceptional, distinctive and extraordinary.

The last purpose found in our corporate identity is for us to become the avenue for His Coming. Because there is a man in heaven, Jesus Christ, the Holy Spirit is now in the earth. It is illegal for any spirit to live on the earth without a body. The Holy Spirit is legally on the earth because He lives among us, in us and through us. The perfect purpose of God is that we are to live not just for the Lord, but as Him. We are to extend our hands as His hands. We are to speak our words as His words. We are to give our love as His love. We are being conformed to His image that we might do His good works and destroy the works of the devil (Acts 10:38).

Therefore before what most believers see as the second coming, He desires to "be-coming again" through our perfected lives to preach, heal, and deliver. The Lord Jesus Christ came as THE Savior, but He calls us to be-coming as His salvation. He is THE Deliverer, but He has purposed us to be-coming as His deliverance to the bound souls in the earth. In the book of Revelation, John the Apostle saw that the kingdoms of this world would become the Kingdom of the Lord and "His" Christ (anointed ones). John the Baptist declared that the Spirit upon Jesus was "without measure. "That same Spirit raised Him (singular) from the dead and has quickened, empowered and purposed our (plural) mortal bodies. The Holy Spirit is without measure or limit upon the corporate body wherein He is always able to anoint, fill up and flow out of one more son who is born into the Kingdom.

The Lord's purpose is perfected in His coming as we become. If we see that His coming is more than His descending from heaven with a final shout (1 Thess. 5:12) but His coming is as we become by opening our lives to reveal Christ in us, the Hope of Glory. The scriptures paint a glorious picture of our corporate identity in Him.

> ➤ In Jude 14 He comes with His saints.
> ➤ In John 14:18, He comes to His saints.
> ➤ In Thessalonians 1:10 He comes in His saints.
> ➤ In Matthew 24:30 He comes in the clouds.
> ➤ In Revelation 1:7 He comes with the clouds.
> ➤ He comes as the lightning.
> ➤ He comes as the morning star.
> ➤ He comes as the sun of righteousness with healing in His wings.
> ➤ He comes as the refiner's fire.
> ➤ He comes in us, to us and through us as Jehovah-Jireh, our provider.
> ➤ He comes as Jehovah-Rophe, our healer.
> ➤ He comes as Jehovah-Shalom, our peace.

HE COMES THROUGH US...WITH PASSION AND PRESENCE

> ➤ He comes as enduringly strong.
> ➤ He comes as entirely sincere.
> ➤ He comes as eternally steadfast.
> ➤ He comes as immortally graceful.
> ➤ He comes as imperially powerful.
> ➤ He comes as impartially merciful.

His passionate purpose? To extend the Father's love in such a way (through us) that those who have not come to the saving knowledge of His presence would receive this wonderful truth.

"For God so loved the world, that he gave his only begotten Son, that whosoever believeth in him should not perish, but have everlasting life. For God sent not his Son into the world to condemn the world; but that the world through him might be saved." (John 3:16-17)

CHAPTER THIRTEEN

Living the Becoming Life

Every father's success truly begins when they begin to see themselves as becoming change agents for the lives of their sons. They must be the catalyst. They must be more like thermostats than thermometers. At first glance, a person could confuse the two. Both are capable of measuring heat. However, they are quite different. The thermometer measures the temperature where the thermostat sets the temperature.

The thermometer is passive. The thermostat is active. The thermometer manages. The thermostat leads. The first records the temperature but can do nothing to change it. The other determines what the environment will be. It effects change in order to set the climate.

The attitude of a spiritual father can be like either one. If the spiritual father is passive then someone else will set the climate of their sons whether they are in ministry or business. If the spiritual father's attitude is active then that attitude will set the climate in which the son lives. A positive attitude and atmosphere will encourage people to accomplish great things.

Throughout my ministry and as a spiritual father I have sought to be a thermostat that sets a positive atmosphere. I believe the atmosphere should be one of faith, hope and love. It should be filled with righteousness, peace and joy. Lifetime learning should not only be encouraged but expected and rewarded. When victories are experienced there should be celebration both privately and publically.

Consistency in this area generates momentum. Many times momentum is the only difference between a winning, positive growth climate and a losing, negative one. Momentum then causes sons to feel better about themselves. They increase their performance and develop appreciation for their Lord, team members and family.

I believe that this appreciation sets the tone for positive expectation.

Some fathers never recognize the importance of creating a climate conducive to building potential sons. They don't understand how the power of climate development. Until they realize this, they will not find true success. The right atmosphere allows potential sons to bloom and grow. That is why the atmosphere needs to be valued and developed first.

When I came to be the Senior Pastor of Christchurch I first began working on creating an environment where people felt encouraged and valued. To see the relationship between environment and growth, look at nature. An observation was made by a man who dives for exotic fish for aquariums. According to him, one of the most popular aquarium fish is the shark. The reason for this is that sharks adapt easily to their environment. It you catch a small shark and confine it, it will stay a size proportionate to the aquarium in which it lives. Sharks can be six inches long and yet fully mature. But turn them loose in the ocean and they will grow to their normal size.

The same is true of potential sons. Some are put into an environment when their sonship quotient is still small, and the confinement of fear, doubt and unbelief causes them to stay small and underdeveloped. Only spiritual fathers can control the environment for the sons around them. They can be the change agents to open up new horizons for growth.

How can a father accomplish this? They must model the sonship they desire. It is a true saying that people do what people see. Part of creating an appealing climate is modeling positive and successful sonship. I believe that spiritual fathers who live a life that others desire to live will draw and connect to people who desire better lives and sonship.

A negative model produces negative results. What the father values, the son will value. The father's goals become their goals. As Lee Iacocca said, "The speed of the boss is the speed of the team." A father cannot demand of others what he does not demand from himself.

As we grow and become sons of God, we need to remember that when people follow us, they can only go as far as we go. If we stop growing, those who follow will do the same. If we stop learning, so will they. Neither personality, theology nor methodology can substitute for a son's personal growth. We cannot model what we do not possess.

Those who believe in our ability do more than stimulate us. They create an atmosphere in which it becomes easier to succeed. The opposite is also true. When a father does not believe in you, success is very difficult for you to achieve. In fact, it becomes nearly impossible.

I try to identify the potential in each future son. I then do my best to cultivate their gifts, talents and abilities in light of their destiny and the needs we have as a church and ministry. This produces a win-win situation. By helping them I am helped. Whatever I sow, I reap. By modeling and mentoring my sons I win because those around me begin to learn, grow and succeed.

Those I lead begin to win because they are being developed, encouraged and blessed.

Great fathers probe those whom they lead for the purpose of finding their desires and dreams. Why? Great fathers know that sons don't care how much you know until they know how much you care. When the father cares about their sons, their needs, their dreams and their desires an atmosphere of love is born.

Once a father is genuinely interested in the well-being of those sons around him, the determination and drive of the sons who follow are activated in a remarkable way. I seek to determine what those who follow me desire the most. Whether it is to be successful in ministry or business I desire their success sometimes more than they initially do. I have found that by believing in the dreams of others their dreams as well as mine becomes reality.

By working to create success in others, others desire success in what we are doing together. It has been amazing to see this work in our East Africa missions ministry. Our church has been a drawing place for those who desire to accomplish great things in the countries of Uganda, Malawi, Kenya and Tanzania. In the past three years I have helped many sons to develop their ministries. I have helped them raise monies as well as teaching them how to be effective in these developing countries.

The result has been so positive even more are now being drawn. Success breeds success. Victory creates more victory.

Some of the qualities every spiritual father should cultivate in their sons are:

1. *Positive Attitude:* This is the ability to work with and see people and situations in a positive way.

2. *Servanthood:* This is the willingness to submit, play team ball and follow others.

3. *Growth Potential:* This is a hunger for personal growth and development; the ability to keep growing as the job expands.

4.   *Follow Through:* The determination to get the job done completely and with consistency.

5.   *Loyalty:* This is the willingness to always put others and the organization above personal desires.

6.   *Resiliency:* This is the ability to bounce back when problems arise.

7.   *Integrity:* Trustworthiness and solid character; consistent words and talk.

8.   *Big Picture Mindset:* This means possessing the ability to see the whole organization and all of its needs.

9.   *Discipline:* This is the willingness to do what is required regardless of personal mood.

10. *Gratitude:* This is about having an attitude of thankfulness that becomes a way of life.

Finally, I work hard to expose every potential son to successful people in their field of work or ministry. I do my best to provide a secure environment where the potential son is free to take risks. This includes helping the potential son find an experienced mentor as well as providing them with the tools and resources to accomplish their purpose. Fathers must learn to spend the time and money to train a potential son in their areas of need.

Accomplishing great things always comes with a price. We must be willing to pay the price to become the sons God desires us to be. The price begins with personal growth. Personal growth requires that we examine ourselves, ask the hard questions about where we are and where we want to be, and then determine to do the right things regardless of atmosphere or mood.

Finally, share yourself and what you have learned with those around you. Pour yourself into others and change their lives. Find conferences and seminars that can pour into you and then take your sons with you. Paying this price will bring you years of fulfillment and joy.

CHAPTER FOURTEEN

What to Look For in a Father

The Lord commissions spiritual fathers, like Abraham, not because of their great oratory, administrative genius or sonship expertise, but because the Lord knows they will correctly and faithfully impart the spiritual pattern given to them in the subsequent generations that follow.

One of the examples in the bible is the prodigal son's father. The parable was told by Jesus in Luke 15. He first spoke of a shepherd who went looking and finding a lost sheep. Next Jesus told of a woman who cleaned and searched her house until she found a coin that had been lost. The last part of the trilogy concerns a son who decides that he no longer needs his father and then asks for and receives his part of the family inheritance. This son strikes out to make his mark in the world only to find that when the money was gone, the friends were gone.

I am convinced the story is more about the father than the son. In Luke 15:20 it says,

"*But while he was still a long way off, his father saw him and was filled with compassion for him; he ran to his son, threw his arms around him and kissed him.*" (Luke 15:20)

The prodigal's father's heart was a giving heart. He had given his son his portion of the inheritance but after it was all spent the father was willing to give again. Like any true spiritual father, he did not give because of what his son could do for him, but rather because the son was in his heart. This father shows us that a son may leave the presence of his father, but he is still in his father's heart.

The prodigal had nothing to give. He had nothing to offer the father except his willingness to become a servant. With a heart full of repentance the son tried his best to become a servant, but the father embraced his grimy body reeking with the stench of the pig pen and hugged him tenaciously so close to his heart that the fragrant anointing of the Spirit exceeded, overwhelmed, and displaced the heartache of the past.

This father then imparted to his son a new identity and inheritance. The robe represents the father's covering and protection. The shoes represent a new path to walk in and a new way of life. Finally, the ring reveals the willingness of the father to trust the son and return to him the authority that had been lost.

The father's view of his son was not contingent upon the son's behavior; it was grounded in steadfast love. The father's view of his son was not based upon the memory of old hurts, but upon ongoing commitment.

I heard Mark Hanby say many years ago, "Warning, don't get too close. The heart of a spiritual father will get a hold of you. He will pull you so close that the anointing on his life will wash away and overcome the odor of a rebellious past. A lost identity and a squandered inheritance will be replaced by a hundred fold blessing of glory and grace."

This kind of a spiritual father has a heart for the sons of God. Like Paul's heart toward Timothy. Paul called Timothy his "beloved son." (1 Timothy 1:2, 2 Timothy 1:2) These words are a term of endearment. The word "beloved" comes from the Greek word: *agaptos* which means beloved, dear, favorite, worthy of love and *teknon* meaning children or offspring.

This is also a term used as a metaphor for the needed intimate and reciprocal relationship that must be formed between a spiritual father and son by the bonds of love, friendship and trust, just as between natural parents and children.

Paul so loved Timothy that the connection lasted all of Paul's life. The strength of the relationship can be seen in Acts 16:3. This is where Paul circumcised Timothy.

The purpose of Timothy's circumcision was not for salvation but for son-ship. This is a true picture that while some become sons from birth others spend somewhere else, but what matters is that a father will be sent from God to find you. Upon finding you, he will begin the process of cutting away that which has kept you from becoming the person God wants you to become.

Paul was so grateful for Timothy. Philippians 2:19-22 reveals the apostle's heart.

"I hope in the Lord Jesus to send Timothy to you soon, that I also may be cheered when I receive news about you. I have no one

*else like him, who takes a genuine interest in your welfare. For
everyone looks out for his own interests, not those of Jesus Christ.
But you know that Timothy has proved himself, because as a son
with his father he has served with me in the work of the gospel."*
What is Paul saying?

➤ He had no one else like Timothy...he had proved himself

➤ Like Paul (his spiritual father) Timothy took a genuine
interest in others

➤ Timothy served Paul as a father in the work of the gospel

Paul also had a father's heart toward the Thessalonians.
In 1 Thessalonians 2:8, 11-12 he wrote,

*"We loved you so much that we were delighted to share with
you not only the gospel of God but our lives as well, because you
had become so dear to us. For you know that we dealt with each of
you as a father deals with his own children, encouraging, comforting
and urging you to live lives worthy of God."*

Here we see that Paul gave his life without holding anything back.
He also used the Greek word *agapêto* (translated "so dear") which is a
term of endearment derived from the language of the nursery. Paul also
encouraged, comforted and urged them as a father.

So in our becoming sons of God, what should we look for in a spiritual
father?

First of all a father should be consistent and faithful in the things of
God. For, if the father is not consistent, what will his sons be? And, if
the father is consistent, what will his sons be?

Secondly, a spiritual father must be consistent in prayer and in the
study of God's Word. He must be consistent in giving of his talent, time
and treasure. This means a spiritual father is to be a role model. 1
Corinthians 11:1 says, *"Be ye followers of me, even as I also am of Christ."*
A role model is a person who serves as an example of the values, attitudes
and behaviors that others admire and want to emulate them.

A spiritual father should be-coming conformed into the image of
Christ. Writing to the Romans, Paul said, *For those God foreknew he also
predestined to be conformed to the likeness of his Son,* (Romans 8:29). This
means that the father should possess a servant spirit, he should be
submitted to authority and successful in ministry.

It is also of utmost importance that a spiritual father be committed
to the training of spiritual sons. The apostle Peter said,

*"So then, those who suffer according to God's will should commit
themselves to their faithful Creator and continue to do good. To the*

elders among you, I appeal as a fellow elder, a witness of Christ's suffering and one who also will share in the glory to be revealed."
(1 Peter 4:19 - 5:1)

A father must be committed to protecting his sons as well as providing for them that which will in the end produce spiritual effectiveness. To do this well a father must have insight and discernment. This is the ability to perceive intuitively the secrets of another's heart, to understand the hidden depths of which the other is unaware. The spiritual father penetrates beneath the conventional gestures and attitudes whereby we conceal our true personality from others and from ourselves; and beyond all these trivialities; he comes to grips with the unique person made in the image and likeness of God. This power is spiritual rather than psychic; it is not simply a kind of extra-sensory perception or a sanctified clairvoyance but the fruit of grace, presupposing concentrated prayer and an unremitting ascetic struggle.

Spiritual fathers should possess the special ability to say the right words and for those words to carry power and authority. His authority must be genuine and must flow out of his personal experience. These types of abilities enable a father to "see" what is ahead in the son's life and what God desires for the son to become.

It is also important for the father to have the giftedness to love sons and make their suffering his own. Loving others involves suffering with and for them; such is the literal sense of compassion found in,

"Bear one another's burdens and so fulfill the law of Christ"
(Galatians 6:2)

The spiritual father is 'the one who *par excellence* bears the burdens of others. A true spiritual father is one who takes a son's soul and will, unto his soul and his will.

It is not enough for him to offer advice. He is also required to take up the soul of his spiritual children into his own soul, their life into his life. It is his task to pray for them, and his constant intercession on their behalf is more important to them than any words of counsel. It is his task likewise to assume their sorrows and their sins, to take their guilt upon himself, and to answer for them before the Lord.

Finally, a spiritual father needs to have the power to introduce spiritual transformation to the son's life. A father can do this by helping his sons to:

➢ Perceive the Kingdom as God created it
➢ Perceive the Church as God wants it to become
➢ Perceive themselves as God wants them to become

➢ Understand there in nothing in God that is trivial

➢ Understand their part in the Kingdom and the Church

Spiritual transformation also comes as a father releases "God's" words to form purpose and potential in the life of the son. The spiritual father does not possess an exhaustive program, neatly worked out in advance and imposed in the same manner upon everyone. On the contrary, if he is a true spiritual father, he will have a different word for each; and since the word which he gives is on the deepest level, not his own but the Holy Spirit's, he does not know in advance what that word will be. But he knows that each word must be designed and designated for the specific son. In reality, the relationship is not two-sided but triangular, for in addition to the father and his son there is also a third partner, God. Our Lord insisted that we should call no man "father," for we have only one father, who is in Heaven (Matthew 13:8-10).

The spiritual father is not an infallible judge or a final court of appeal, but a fellow-servant of the living God; not a dictator, but a guide and companion on the way. The only true "spiritual director," in the fullest sense of the word, is the Holy Spirit. What the spiritual father gives to his son is not a code of written or oral regulations, not a set of techniques for meditation, but a personal relationship. Within this personal relationship the spiritual father grows and changes as well as the son, for God is constantly guiding them both. He may on occasion provide detailed verbal instructions, with precise answers to specific questions. On other occasions he may fail to give any answer at all; either because he does not think that the question needs an answer, or because he himself does not yet know what the answer should be.

But these answers—or this failure to answer—are always given the framework of a personal relationship. Many things cannot be said in words, but can be conveyed through a direct personal encounter.

Many people have the idea that they cannot find a spiritual father, because they expect him to be of a particular type: they want an Apostle Paul, and so they close their eyes to the fathers whom God is actually sending to them. Often their supposed problems are not so very complicated, and in reality they already know in their own heart what the answer is. But they do not like the answer, because it involves patient and sustained effort on their part: and so they look for a *father like Moses or Elijah or Paul* who, by a single miraculous word, will suddenly make everything easy. A spiritual father is not given to make our lives easier, but better. Spiritual fathers impart understanding of the true nature of spiritual direction of growing and maturing in Christ Jesus.

CHAPTER FIFTEEN

Finding Your Spiritual Father

Relationships between fathers and sons are a key to the Kingdom of God. The Lord wants to bring the young and the old together, bind them close to each other and to their God, and teach them to build His Kingdom together. God's Kingdom is created and established through the spirit of adoption or sonship:

1. Through enlargement as new sons are added to the Kingdom.
2. Through advancement as sons are brought to maturity in their relationship with God and others.

This advancement happens when God's people embrace the spirit of adoption which communicates the key ideas of the process of maturity. This process develops and encourages people as they walk the path of becoming mature and enabled to spiritually "father" themselves.

The core essentials to the spirit of adoption are:

God attaches the person with a need to the person with the resources to meet that need. When He does this both persons must be willing to develop relationship with the other. The "son" must be willing to be empowered by the father and willing to receive the resources the father has in his possession.

The spiritual father may be sent by God to meet these needs of the son for a situation…a season…a generation…a lifetime. The father must be willing and able to instruct, inform, instigate and impart into the life of the son. The goal must be to model, mentor, maximize and magnify the son helping the son to overcome the obstacles in his life and ministry.

Spiritual fathering is not gender specific but help specific. Fathering empowers a son to negotiate obstacles, reach their potential, and prepare for ministry. This comes as the father imparts knowledge, wisdom and anointing as well as modeling character and integrity.

The spiritual fathering or parenting process has at its core the intention of raising healthy sons who can produce more productive and healthy sons. This is also the hearts cry of a spiritual father. His goal is for his sons to reach their full potential as men and women of God. In a spiritual parenting relationship, all of this takes place in an atmosphere of patient love and acceptance, without judgment or fear of gossip. It is meant to happen naturally and easily by example and modeled behavior as a spiritual father imparts his blessing to his spiritual children.

Fathers must learn to impart all that the Lord has taught them. It is not about age, but experience. The adopted son must look for a father willing to go before them as well as a father willing to share what they have. It is important that sons value the journey of their fathers and are willing to follow them as they follow Christ.

The relational interchange within the spirit of adoption is mutually beneficial to father and son, creating an environment of blessed enrichment. The depth of this spiritual relationship releases a synergistic energy for the adoptee not attainable on their own.

Mark Hanby said, "A spiritual father is the one whose words pierced beyond the veneer of a blessing into the very heart and marrow of your existence, causing a massive realignment to your spirit. A spiritual father is not necessarily the one who birthed you into the kingdom. Instead, he is the one who rescues you from the doorstop of your abandonment and receives you into his house, gives you a name, and makes you his son."

The spirit of adoption works in the life of a son when they find a father who will "see" their potential and purpose. This kind of father will believe in the son more than the son does. This faith will "draw out" what God has placed in the son and give the father the ability to tolerate immaturity for the sake of producing a righteous seed. A true spiritual father:

1. Will have the ability to tolerate certain things
2. Will love you as you are
3. Will love you so much to not let you stay who you are
4. Will polish you as to remove the rough edges
5. Will possess the encouragement you need
6. Will deliver the positive criticism you need
7. Will find faith instead of fault
8. Will be able to see the big picture with you in it.

Good spiritual fathers see the big picture. Seeing the big picture is the ability to see down the long road, taking into account the whole of the issue instead of just a small portion, thus, maintaining balance and perspective. A father with perspective can make helpful suggestions, bring up points that would otherwise not be considered, and help the adoptee take more information into consideration.

There are eight hindrances adoptees must overcome to receiving the resources from a father.

Ignorance—having not heard of spiritual fathering or not understanding the concept. God is a Father to the fatherless (Psalm 68:5). When we understand that God is a God of families and wants each person simply "grow up" to be a spiritual adult so they can help another person(s), we understand spiritual fathering.

Apathy—being wrapped up in one's own life and selfish desires and becoming apathetic toward the things of God. We must be willing to include room for a spiritual father in our daily lives. Spiritual sons learn much more by watching a father live his life in Christ before them than by listening to great "sermons."

Insecurity—not feeling adequate. The paralysis of insecurity prevents movement beyond the comfort zone. Adoptees must overcome their own insecurity and "reveal" their true selves to the father God has placed in their lives.

Timidity—waiting on the sidelines due to lack of a natural or spiritual role model. God, the perfect Father, is the role model who loves us. He believes the best about us. We must allow Him to send fathers into our lives and then be willing to participate with them.

Impatience—quitting when quick results are not seen. It is often hard work for spiritual fathers or mothers to nurture and train spiritual babies before they can grow up to care for themselves and eventually become spiritual adults. Perseverance and dependency upon the Lord are essential. Don't quit!

Fear of making mistakes—Just as mistakes are made in natural parenting, so it will happen in spiritual parenting. Working through the struggles and mistakes with transparency and honesty provides opportunities for growth and authenticity.

Hurts from the past—getting hurt in the process of spiritual parenting and not wanting to be hurt again. The immature, inconsistent, irritating behaviors of spiritual children struggling to come to maturity will more than likely cause some pain and disappointment for the father and the son. Rather than count it against the other, we must continue to be consistent, lovingly gentle, lean wholly on the Lord, and trust the Lord to raise us up His way.

Abuse of authority—warping the entire concept of spiritual fathers. Healthy spiritual fathers earn the right to speak into their sons' lives because they do so with the heart of a servant, affirming and encouraging them in their walk with Christ. A level of trust is built over time in a balanced relationship that encourages sons and daughters to be dependent on God.

Godly fathers want to serve others, and treat all men and women as their equals. Their actions proceed from an attitude of equality, not authority, because they are more concerned with serving than ruling.

The following chart helps point out the differences between the two approaches:

Dominating Fathers:	*True Fathers in the Lord:*
1. Function as if they are The source of guidance for people's lives.	1. Believe that God is the source of guidance and desire to help other Christians to learn His voice.
2. Emphasize the rights of sons.	2. Emphasize the responsibilities of sons.
3. Set sons apart and give them special privileges.	3. Emphasize the body of Christ serving one another.
4. Seek to control people's actions.	4. Encourage people to be dependant on God.
5. Emphasize the importance of the sons ministering to others.	5. Emphasize the importance of equipping the saints for the work of the ministry.
6. Use rules and laws to control people and force them to conform to a mold.	6. Provide an atmosphere of trust and grace to encourage growth.

Every spiritual son should seek to find a true father. Pray the Lord to either bring such a father into your life or reveal such a person who is already in your life. Ask him to consider being a father to your life. Ask if he has a "spiritual life coach" or "fathering" program you can be a part of. Offer your help and service in return for his time.

Then take the following ten steps...

1. Receive the spirit of adoption.

"For you did not receive a spirit that makes you a slave again to fear, but you received the Spirit of sonship. (Or adoption) And by him we cry, "Abba, (Aramaic for Father) Father." (Romans 8:15)

2. Forgive a father who has abandoned or abused you.

"And when you stand praying, if you hold anything against anyone, forgive him, so that your Father in heaven may forgive you your sins." (Mark 11:25)

3. Be willing to be attached to the father God sends.

"It is right for me to feel this way about all of you, since I have you in my heart; for whether I am in chains or defending and confirming the gospel, all of you share in God's grace with me." (Philippians 1:7)

4. Accept him as you would the Lord Jesus Christ.

"I tell you the truth, whoever accepts anyone I send accepts me; and whoever accepts me accepts the one who sent me." (John 13:20)

5. Ask the Lord to remove all hindrances.

"You do not have, because you do not ask God. When you ask, you do not receive, because you ask with wrong motives, that you may spend what you get on your pleasures." (James 4:2-3)

6. Submit to his sonship and guidance.

"Moreover, we have all had human fathers who disciplined us and we respected them for it. How much more should we submit to the Father of our spirits and live!" (Hebrews 12:9)

7. Refuse to stay immature no matter how hard the struggle.

"Endure hardship as discipline; God is treating you as sons. For what son is not disciplined by his father?" (Hebrews 12:7)

8. Show appreciation verbally and financially.

"Anyone who receives instruction in the word must share all good things with his instructor." (Galatians 6:6)

9. Honor your father privately and publicly.

"A student is not above his teacher, but everyone who is fully trained will be like his teacher." (Luke 6:40)

"Honor your father and mother"-- which is the first commandment with a promise--"that it may go well with you and that you may enjoy long life on the earth." (Ephesians 6:2-3)

10. Grow and Mature in the things of God.

"Then we will no longer be infants, tossed back and forth by the waves, and blown here and there by every wind of teaching and by

the cunning and craftiness of men in their deceitful scheming. Instead, speaking the truth in love, we will in all things grow up into him who is the Head, that is, Christ. From him the whole body, joined and held together by every supporting ligament, grows and builds itself up in love, as each part does its work." (Ephesians 4:11-16)

God's word in Malachi 4:6 tells us that in the end time he will turn the hearts of the fathers to the children and the hearts of the children to the fathers. Yes, this applies to the natural parent-child relationship, but bible scholars say that the literal translation of the verse means those who are mature in the things of God loving, training and disciplining those who are young in the Lord.

They have counted the cost that having this kind of relationship would mean to them emotionally, physically and spiritually. But despite any hardship on themselves, they have chosen to affect the Kingdom of God by spiritually mentoring and loving those who are young in the ways of the God kind of life.

True spiritual fathers follow the example of Jesus Christ; they are not content to love only on a surface level. They are willing to pay the personal price to raise up a new generation of sons and daughters for the Kingdom of heaven. May we take our place following those called to raise up the next generation and repair the breach between God and man.

CONCLUSION

Now We Are the Sons of God

"Behold, what manner of love the Father hath bestowed upon us, that we should be called the sons of God: therefore the world knoweth us not, because it knew him not. Beloved, now are we the sons of God, and it doth not yet appear what we shall be: but we know that, when he shall appear, we shall be like him; for we shall see him as he is." (1 John 3:1-2)

The Kingdom of God is based upon relationship, and the central relationship is one of parent to child - father to son.

"Older women. should admonish the younger women" (Titus 2:4)

"Timothy, my true son in the faith" (1 Tim.1:2)

"I am your father in the gospel" (1 Cor. 4:15)

We stay spiritually immature when those who are called by God to care for us abandon us, or when those who should care, do not.We may have an orphan spirit because of the natural parenting we received.Perhaps you were literally abandoned, or abused. Perhaps you had an absent father, or abusive mother. Perhaps you raised yourself because of the financial condition of your family, or the number of children in the home.

On the spiritual side, neglect happens at every level in institutional Christianity. Sons demand instead of admonish, berate instead of beseech, are busy with church life instead of the life inside the people, and are not being fathered by the system themselves. There are promises of parental love, but in reality, scarce little more than an attempt to parent from a distance.

Father and son relationships should not be a kick or trend, but a pioneering standard of excellence which helps ensures the legacy of life transcending and imparting the presence of God from father to son.The true nature of a spiritual father-son relationship is that the Lord is the one that appoints and directs, He is the Lord of Relationships. No legislation, no compulsion of any human ingenuity, or lording over one's conscience, and no inferiority complexes.

To begin a relationship out of inordinate fear is unhealthy. To attempt to walk in an appointed relationship out of lingering anger and hostility is unhealthy. Yet a number of folks are out there utilizing these limited inner resources to respond in the manner that they are. Suspicious, loaded questioning, and not valuing the true counsel and covenant of The Father's Spirit.

Father-son relationships are not about having a covering or canopy over your life and ministry. Paul the apostle did not teach covering, he taught relationship. The apostles did not teach generic ordination, but recognition of those whom the Lord would divinely appoint. God is not trying to cover us up, but to uncover if you will, and then recover our lives with His self.

For people who haven't been adjusted into this new Kingdom configuration, I would suggest that you define and add new meaning to the word father and son relationship by looking beyond the old patterns of how you are used to seeing things done, or not done, and to access and to extract a new understanding that is really buried deep within the heart of God.

Now heritage or inheritance is not alone confined to what one can give you materially, but a true covenantal heritage is intangible, and priceless. It may be the simple passing on of a good name, lifetime core values, and a significant progression in life. Truth told any inheritance should be life changing and life-giving in nature.It should grow in instances of time, becoming interwoven throughout a lifetime, and multiply into spiritual generations ages and ages to come. Thus, the legacy of life, is what destiny produces, and legacy re-produces.

Do not let the whispering experiences of the past alter your perception nor rob you of a glorious and rewarding future by bringing up the fear of intimacy, fear of failure, or fear of the unknown. If you ask for bread the Lord will not give you a stone.The Heavenly Father knows what we need when we ask Him, and in many cases, our needed breakthrough is hinged upon someone coming into our life to speak into our progression.

If we say we believe in apostolic fathers of the Spirit, yet perceive the one we have relationship with to only to agree with our immaturity or be negligent in causing us to grow up spiritually, then we need new fathers who will step up and challenge our way of life and ministry.

After today, you might still sometimes hear the last desperate gasps of that old voice trying to draw you back into your old negative and religious life. You might still hear the voice of fear that guided you down so many lonely roads. But now you have found something new. *Sonship…The art of becoming a son.*

You will never again have to listen to those old voices or travel the old paths. You have found the right road. The Lord will help you to have the courage to continue onward and upward toward finding a spiritual father who will love you, nurture you, respect you and help you become all God has destined you to be.

By learning to submit to scriptural order (also called the spirit of adoption in Romans chapter eight) you will experience the power of God described by Paul to the Colossians.

From now on, your becoming will be, "rooted, built up and established in the faith of the Son of God."

About Robert Stone

For more than 38 years, the ministry of Robert and Susan Stone has been primarily focused on establishing the Kingdom of God in the earth. Quietly, yet effectively, Robert and Susan have been working around the world in the Name of Jesus bringing love, light and life to the most troubled and needy areas.

The Stones are committed to model the ministry of Jesus and make every effort to do good works in His name. Robert and Susan are currently pastoring Christchurch in Tulsa, Oklahoma. Robert began preaching at the age of fourteen. He and Susan traveled throughout the United States and overseas for over twenty years before establishing and overseeing several churches throughout North and South America.

Through their partnership with people from all over the world, the Stone's ministry now has ministries serving the poorest of the poor in many parts of the world, touching thousands of lives each day. Conferences and seminars continue to be held throughout Tanzania, Kenya, Uganda, Rwanda, Malawi, Zambia and Burundi in East Africa. Construction of Tanzania Destiny Center is now underway near Mt. Kilimanjaro, Tanzania, East Africa.

The vision for the training center in northern Tanzania, East Africa is to establish group homes for orphaned children, provide medical care for thousands of the nomadic Masai tribe, teach business leadership and development as well as help train 5,000 pastors with the capability to lead their congregations in the pattern of God for discipleship: The Principle of Twelve. By reaching this goal, the Stones will be able to help over a million people in the countries of East Africa.

This is of great personal significance to them. When many said that it would be too difficult to reach out to those in faraway lands with the message of the gospel...Robert and Susan chose to believe God rather than man. They now have constructed 38 churches and four bible schools that continue to impact multitudes in nations throughout the world. The Stones also continue to obey the Word of God and send support to starving children and homeless widows in war torn countries.

Robert has also written five other bestselling books, *Ordering Your Steps, Gifts from the Ascended Christ, The Principle of Twelve; the Pattern of God and Finding Financial Freedom*. His newest book prior to this one, *Pursuing Perfection*, was released in late August 2009.

For more information concerning the Stone's ministry please contact:

Telephone: (918) 599-9319

Email: info@destinyreformation.com

Website: www.destinyreformation.com
Website: www.bishoprobertstone.com

Church: Christchurch
3 South 41st West Ave.
Tulsa, OK 74127

Mailing address: PO Box 330118
Tulsa, OK 74133

Made in the USA
Charleston, SC
21 November 2010